Vintage Gardening

Vintage Gardening

ÉDITIONS
PLACE DES
VICTOIRES

KÖNEMANN

KÖNEMANN

© 2019 koenemann.com GmbH

www.koenemann.com

ÉDITIONS
PLACE DES
VICTOIRES

© Éditions Place des Victoires

6, rue du Mail – 75002 Paris

www.victoires.com

Dépôt légal : 3ᵉ trimestre 2019

ISBN: 978-2-8099-1700-0

Series Concept: koenemann.com GmbH

Responsible Editor: Jenny Tiesler

Text: GAP Photos Ltd

Translations: koenemann.com GmbH

Layout: Oliver Hessmann, Christoph Eiden

Colour Separation: Prepress, Cologne

Picture credits: GAP Photos Ltd

ISBN: 978-3-7419-2363-0

Printed in China by Shyft Publishing / Hunan Tianwen Xinhua Printing Co., Ltd

Content · Sommaire · Inhalt · Índice · Inhoud

Setting in scene
Mise en scène
In Szene gesetzt
Llevado a escena
Messa in scena
In scène zetten

Edinburgh, Scotland

A *Dianthus carthusianorum*	**B** *Lavandula*	**C** *Delphinium*	**D** *Rosa*	**F** *Centranthus ruber*	**G** *Geranium*
Carthusian Pink	Lavender	Larkspur	Rose	Red Valerian	Cranesbill
Œillet des chartreux	Lavande	Dauphinelle	Rosier	Centranthe rouge	Géranium
Karthäusernelke	Lavendel	Rittersporn	Roos	Rote Spornblume	Storchschnabel
Garofanino dei Certosini	Lavanda	Espuela del caballero		Valeriana roja	Geranio
Kartuizer anjer		Delfinio	**E** *Penstemon*	Valeriana rossa	Ooievaarsbek
		Ridderspoor	Bartfaden	Rode valeriaan	
			Campanitas		
			Schildpadbloem		

Mortola, Italy

A *Geranium*	**B** *Achillea millefolium subsp. sudetica*	**C** *Bellis perennis*	**D** *Pulmonaria*
Cranesbill	Yarrow	Common Daisy	Lungwort
Géranium	Achillées	Pâquerette	Pulmonaire
Storchschnabel	Gemeine Schafgarbe	Tausenschön	Lungenkraut
Geranio	Milenrama	Margarita común	Hoja del pulmón
Ooievaarsbek	Achillea	Margheritina	Longkruid
	Duizendblad	Madeliefje	

A *Capsicum annuum*
Pepper
Piment d'ornement
Paprika
Pimiento
Peperone

B *Petroselinum*
Parsley
Persil
Petersilie
Perejil
Prezzemolo
Peterselie

C *Dahlia*
Dahlie

Saffron Walden, UK

A *Hydrangea anomala* *subsp petiolaris*	**B** *Lupinus*	**C** *Buxus*	**D** *Geranium* *Armeria maritima*	**E** *Digitali*
Climbing Hydrangea	Lupin	Box	Thrift	Foxglove
Hortensia grimpant	Lupine	Buis	Armérie maritime	Digitale
Kletterhortensie	Lupinus	Buchsbaum	Strand-Grasnelke	Roter Fingerhu
Hortensia trepadora	Lupine	Boj	Clavelina de mar	Dedalera
Ortensia petiolaris		Bosso	Engels gras	Digitale
Klimhortensia		Buksboom		Vingerhoedskrui

A
B
C
D

A *Chrysanthemum*
Chrysanthème
Chrysantheme
Crisantemos
Crisantemo
Chrysant

B *Cucurbita*
Pumpkin
Citrouille
Kürbis
Calabaza gigante
Zucca
Pompoen

C *Viola*
Pansy
Pensée
Stiefmütterchen
Pensamiento
Viola del pensiero
Viooltje

D *Sempervivum*
Houseleek
Joubarbe
Hauswurz
Siemprevivas
Semprevivo
Huislook

A *Rudbeckia fulgida*
Orange coneflower
Rudbéckie lumineuse
Leuchtender Sonnenhut
Margherita gialla
Gele zonnehoed

B *Lysimachia nummularia 'Aurea'*

Creeping Jenny
Herbes aux écus
Gelbes Pfennigkraut
Planta de la moneda
Penningkruid

C *Sempervivum*
Houseleek
Joubarbe
Hauswurz
Siemprevivas
Semprevivo
Huislook

D *Canna*
Canna
Balisier
Blumenrohr
Bloemriet

E *Begonia × tuberhybrida*
Begonia
Bégonia tubéreux
Knollenbegonie
Begonia tuberosa
Knolbegonia

F *Euphorbia hypericifolia*
'Diamond Frost'
Baby's Breath Euphorbia
Euphorbes
Zauberschnee
Hierba de la golondrina
Euphorbia
Wolfsmelk

A *Saponaria officinalis*
Saponaria
Saponaire
Gewöhnliches Seifenkraut
Saponaria comune
Zeepkruid

B *Rodgersia*
Schaublatt
Schout-bij-nacht

C *Echeveria cante*
Hen and Chicks
Écheveria
Echeverie
Rosa de alabastro
Echeveria cante

D *Hosta*
Plantain Lilly
Hosta
Herzblattlilie
Planta de lidia
Hartlelie

A *Cucurbita*	**B** *Solanum lycopersicum*	**C** *Tropaeolum*	**D** *Pelargonium*	**E** *Capsicum annuum*
Squash	Tomato	Nasturtium	Geranium	Pepper
Courge plutôt que potimarron	Tomate	Capucine	Pélargonium	Piment d'ornement
Kürbis	Pomodoro	Kapuzinerkresse	Pelargonie	Paprika
Pompoen	Tomaat	Capuchina	Geranio	Pimiento
		Nasturzio	Ooievaarsbek	Peperone
		Oost-Indische kers		

A *Acer palmatum*

Japanese Maple
Érable palmé
Fächerahorn
Arce japonés palmeado
Acero palmato
Japanse esdoorn

B *Lobelia*

Lobélie
Lobelie

C *Petunia*

Pétunia
Petunie

D *Pelargonium*

Geranium
Pélargonium
Pelargonie
Geranio
Ooievaarsbek

E *Calibrachoa*

Million Bells
Zauberglöckchen
Petunia calibrachoa
Petunia nana
Minipetunia

F *Sedum*

Stonecrop
Orpin
Fetthenne
Hierba callera
Borracina
Vetkruid

G *Dahlia × hortensis*

Dahlie
Dahlia

H *Acer campestre*
Field Maple
Érable champêtre
Feldahorn
Arce silvestre
Acero di campo
Veldesdoorn

I *Chrysanthemum*
Chrysanthème
Chrysantheme
Crisantemo
Chrysant

A *Sempervivum*
Houseleek
Joubarbe
Hauswurz
Siemprevivas
Semprevivo
Huislook

B *Parthenocissus tricuspidata*
Boston Ivy
Vigne-vierge à trois pointes
Dreispitzige Jungfernrebe
Viña trepadora
Vite americana
Oosterse wingerd

C *Sedum reflexum*
Reflexed stonecrop
Orpin réfléchi
Felsen-Fetthenne
Siempreviva
Borracina rupestre
Tripmadam

A *Hydrangea macrophylla*
Bigleaf Hydrangea
Hortensia
Gartenhortensie
Hortensia
Ortensia dei fioristi

B *Papaver cambricum*
Welsh Poppy
Pavot du Pays
de Galles
Wald-Scheinmohn
Amapola amarilla
Papavero cambricum
Schijnpapaver

C *Dianthus barbatus*
Sweet William
Œillet de poète
Bartnelke
Clavel del poeta
Garofano dei poeti
Duizendschoon

D *Geranium*
macrorrhizum
'Bevan's Variety'
Bulgarian Geranium
Géranium à
grosses racines
Balkan-
Storchschnabel
Geranio
Rotsooievaarsbek

E *Trifolium repens*
Claver
Trèfle
Weißklee
Trifolium
Trifoglio bianco
Klaver

F *Geranium*
maderense
Giant Herb Robert
Géranium de Madère
Madeira-
Storchschnabel
Geranio maderense
Ooievaarsbek

East Sussex, UK

Hertfordshire, UK

London, UK

A *Sempervivum calcareum*

Houseleek

Joubarbe du calcaire

Kalk-Hauswurz

Siemprevivas

Semprevivo del calcare

Huislook

B *Sempervivum arachnoideum*

Cobweb houseleek

Joubarbe à toile d'araignée

Spinnweb-Sempervivum

Siemprevivas

Semprevivo ragnateloso

Huislook

C *Sempervivum montanum*

Mountain houseleek

Joubarbe des montagnes

Berg-Hauswurz

Semprevivo montano

Berghuislook

Greenwich Village, New York City, USA

A *Rosmarinus officinalis*
Rosemary
Romarin officinal
Rosmarin
Romero
Rosmarino
Rozemarijn

B *Solanum lycopersicum 'Tumbling Tom Red'*
Tomato
Tomate
Pomodoro
Tomaat

A *Hedera colchica*
Persian Ivy
Lierre de Perse
Kaukasischer Efeu
Hiedra persa
Edera Dentata
Variegata
Klimop

B *Calibrachoa*
Million Bells
Zauberglöckchen
Petunia calibrachoa
Petunia nana
Minipetunia

C *Geranium*
Cranesbill
Géranium
Storchschnabel
Geranio
Ooievaarsbek

D *Fuchsia*
Fuchsie
Pendientes
de la reina
Fucsia
Bellenplant

Melbourne, Australia

A *Aloe arborescens*
Candelabra Aloe
Aloès
Baum-Aloe
Aloe candelabro
Aloe arborescens
Aloë

B *Tagetes erecta*
French Marigold
Roses d'Inde
Studentenblume
Damasquina
Tagete
Afrikaantje

C *Haworthia fasciata*
Haworthia
Haworthie

NOS BONS PETITS OISEAUX

Floral vintage decoration
Décoration florale vintage
Nostalgische Blumendeko
Decoración floral nostálgica
Decorazione floreale nostalgica
Vintage bloemdecoraties

South Africa

Berkshire, UK

A *Calibrachoa*
Million Bells
Zauberglöckchen
Petunia calibrachoa
Petunia nana
Minipetunia

B *Pelargonium*
Geranium
Pélargonium
Pelargonie
Geranio

C *Clematis*
Clématite
Waldrebe
Clemátide
Clematide
Bosrank

D *Lysimachia punctata*
Variegated
Loosestrife
Lysimaque ponctuée
Punktierter
Gilbweiderich
Mazza d'oro
punteggiata
Puntwederik

E *Primula polyantha*
Primrose
Primevère polyanthus
Stängellose
Schlüsselblume
Prímula polyanthus
Primula polyantha
Sleutelbloem

A *Galanthus nivalis*
Snowdrop
Perce-neige
Schneeglöckchen
Galanto
Bucaneve
Sneeuwklokje

B *Helleborus*
Lenten Rose
Hellébore
Christrose
Eléboro
Elleboro
Kerstroos

A *Geranium × johnsonii*
Cranesbill
Géranium
Storchschnabel
Geranio
Ooievaarsbek

B *Aquilegia vulgaris alba*
European Columbine
Ancolie
Akelei
Aquilegia

C *Rosa 'Blush Noisette'*
Rose
Rosier
Roos

D *Rosa*
Rose
Rosier
Roos

E *Aquilegia vulgaris*
European Columbine
Ancolie
Akelei
Aquilegia

F *Akebia quinata*
Chocolate Vine
Akébie à cinq feuilles
Fingerblättrige Akebie/
Schokoladenwein
Aquebia
Akebia a cinque foglie
Schijnaugurke

G *Stachys byzantina*
Lambs Ear
Épiaire de Byzance
Wollziest
Oreja de liebre
Orecchio d'agnello
Ezelsoor

A *Ocimum basilicum*
Basil
Basilic
Basilikum
Albahaca
Basilico
Basilicum

B *Viola odorata*
Sweet Violet
Violette odorante
Duftveilchen
Violeta común
Viola mammola
Maarts viooltje

A *Aquilegia*
European Columbine
Ancolie
Akelei
Aquilegia

B *Myosotis*
Forget-Me-Not
Myosotis
Vergissmeinnicht
Nomeolvides
Nontiscordardimé
Vergeet-mij-nietje

C *Digitalis*
Foxglove
Digitale
Fingerhut
Dedalera
Digitale
Vingerhoedskruid

D *Osteospermum*
African Daisy
Marguerite africaine
Kapkörbchen
Spaanse margriet

E *Hedera helix*
Ivy
Lierre grimpant
Efeu
Hiedra común
Edera comune
Klimop

London, UK

Ontario, Canada

London, UK

South Yorkshire, UK

A *Rosa 'Niphetos'*
Rose
Rosier
Roos

B *Geranium*
Cranesbill
Géranium
Storchschnabel
Geranio
Ooievaarsbek

A *Alchemilla mollis*

Ladys Mantle

Manteau de
Notre-Dame

Weicher
Frauenmantel

Capa de señora
mollis

Erba stella

Vrouwenmantel

B *Matthiola incana*

Stocks

Grande giroflée

Garten-Levkoje

Matthiola incana

Violacciocca rossa

Zomerviolier

C *Argyranthemum
frutescens*

Marguerite Daisy

Chrysanthème
frutescent

Strauchmargerite

Margarita

Margherita
delle Canarie

Struikmargriet

D *Rosa 'New Dawn'*

Rose

Rosier

Roos

E *Viola odorata*
Sweet Violet
Violette odorante
Duftveilchen
Violeta común
Viola mammola
Maarts viooltje

Maritime ideas
Idées maritimes
Maritime Ideen
Ideas marítimas
Idee marittime
Maritieme ideeën

A *Lysimachia punctata*	**B** *Erigeron karvinskianus*	**C** *Lavandula angustifolia 'Hidcote'*	**D** *Senecio cineraria*	**E** *Limonium*	**F** *Festuca glauca*
Spotted Loosestrife	Mexican Fleabane	English Lavender	Silver Ragwort	Sea Lavender	Blue Fescue
Lysimaque ponctuée	Vergerette de Karvinski	Lavande à feuilles étroites	Séneçon cinéraire	Strandflieder	Fétuque bleue
Punktierter Gilbweiderich	Mexikanisches Berufskraut	Echter Lavendel	Silber-Greiskraut	Limonio	Blau-Schwingel
Lisimaquia punteada	Margarita cimarrona	Espliego	Jacobaea maritima	Lamsoor	Festuca azulada
Mazza d'oro punteggiata	Cespica karvinskiana	Lavanda officinale	Cineraria marittima		Festuca azzurra
Puntwederik	Muurfijnstraal	Echte lavendel	Kruiskruid		Blauw schapengras

Cowes, Isle of Wight, UK

A *Senecio cineraria*
Silver Ragwort
Séneçon
Silber-Greiskraut
Senecio
Cineraria marittima
Kruiskruid

B *Erigeron karvinskianus*
Mexican Fleabane
Vergerette de Karvinski
Mexikanisches Berufskraut
Margarita cimarrona
Cespica karvinskiana
Muurfijnstraal

C *Nicotinana*
Tobacco Plants
Nicotiana
Tabakpflanze
Tabaco de Virginia
Nicotinana
Tabaksplant

D *Festuca glauca*
Blue Fescue
Fétuque bleue
Blau-Schwingel
Festuca azulada
Festuca azzurra
Blauw schapengras

A *Lupinus*
Lupin
Lupine
Lupino

B *Primula bulleyana*
Bulley's Primrose
Primevère candélabre
Etagen-Schlüsselblume
Sleutelbloem

C *Prunus*
Cherry
Cerisier
Kirsche
Ciliegio
Kers

D *Cistus*
Ciste
Zistrose
Jara
Cisto
Cistusroosje

E *Thymus*
Thyme
Thym
Thymian
Tomillo
Timo
Tijm

F *Rosa*
Rose
Rosier
Roos

G *Geranium*
Cranesbill
Géranium
Storchschnabel
Geranio
Ooievaarsbek

H *Hydrangea paniculata*
Hydrangea
Hortensia
Rispen-Hortensie
Hortensias
Ortensia paniculata

East Sussex, UK

A *Rosa*
Rose
Rosier
Roos

B *Primula auricula*
Auricula
Oreille d'Ours
Aurikel
Primula orecchia d'orso

C *Thymus*
Thyme
Thym
Thymian
Tomillo
Timo
Tijm

Essex, UK

A *Heuchera*
Alum Root
Heuchère
Purpurglöckchen
Campanillas de coral
Purperklokje

B *Iris*
Schwertlilie
Lis

C *Zaluzianskya ovata*
Night Phlox
Phlox de nuit
Sternbalsam
Nachtflox

D *Tradescantia*
Spiderwort
Misère
Dreimasterblumen/
Gottesauge
Amor de hombre
Erba miseria
Vaderplant

E *Rosa*	**F** *Helleborus*	**G** *Geranium*	**H** *Santolina chamaecyparissus*	**I** *Iris pallida*
Rose	Lenten Rose	Cranesbill	Cotton Lavender	Dalmatian Iris
Rosier	Hellébore	Géranium	Santoline petit-cyprès	Iris pâle
Roos	Christrose	Storchschnabel	Graues Heiligenkraut	Bleiche Schwertlilie
	Eléboro	Geranio	Abrótano hembra	Iris dulce
	Elleboro	Ooievaarsbek	Crespolina Corsa	Giaggiolo
	Kerstroos		Heiligenbloem	Iris pallida

A *Oenothera biennis*
Evening primrose
Onagre bisannuelle
Gemeine Nachtkerze
Onagra común
Enagra comune
Middelste
teunisbloem

B *Kniphofia*
Red Hot Pokers
Kniphofia
Fackellilie
Tizón de fuego
Kniphofia
Vuurpijl

C *Sedum*
Stonecrop
Orpin
Fetthenne
Hierba callera
Borracina
Vetkruid

D *Eryngium*
Sea Holly
Panicault
Mannstreu
Cardo
Eryngium
Kruisdistel

E *Verbascum chaixii*
Mullein
Molène de Chaix
Österreich-
Königskerze
Berbasco
Verbasco di Chaix
Toorts

F *Echinops*
Globe Thistle
Chardon bleu
Kugeldistel
Kogeldistel

G *Limonium*
   platyphyllum
Sea Lavender
Lavande de Mer
Strandflieder
Limonium
platyphyllum
Limonium
platyphyllum
Lamsoor

H *Morina longifolia*
Himalayan
Whorlflower
Morina Longifolia
Langblättrige
Kardendistel
Morina longifolia
Morina longifolia
Kransbloem

I *Knautia arvensis*
Field Scabious
Knautie des champs
Acker-Witwenblume
Viuda silvestre
Ambretta
Beemdkroon

J *Foeniculum vulgare*
Fennel
Fenouil commun
Fenchel
Hinojo
Finocchio
Venkel

K *Cytisus scoparius*
Common Broom
Cytise
Besenginster
Cytisus
Citiso
Brem

89

East Sussex, UK

A *Trachycarpus fortunei*
Chinese Windmill Palm
Palmier de Chine
Chinesische Hanfpalme
Palmera excelsa
Palma cinese
Henneppalm

B *Aloe*
Aloès
Aloë

C *Crambe maritima*
Sea Kale
Crambe maritime
Echter Meerkohl
Col marina
Cavolo marino
Zeekool

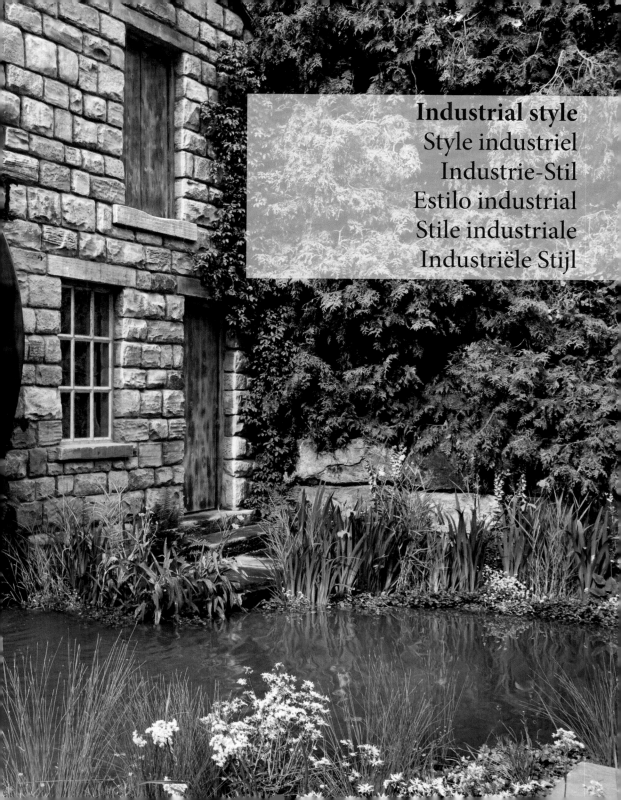

Industrial style
Style industriel
Industrie-Stil
Estilo industrial
Stile industriale
Industriële Stijl

A *Hosta 'Halycon'*

Plantain Lilly
Hosta
Herzblattlilie
Planta de lidia
Hartlelie

B *Persicaria microcephala 'Red Dragon'*

Knotweeds
Renouée microcéphale
Kleinkopfiger Knöterich
Persicaria
Duizendknoop

C *Equisetum hyemale*

Rough horsetail
Prêle d'hiver
Winter-Schachtelhalm
Equiseto de invierno
Equiseto invernale
Schaafstro

D *Imperata cylindrica 'Rubra'*

Cogon Grass
Impérate cylindrique
Japanisches Blutgras
Marciega
Erba del sangue giapponese
Japans bloedgras

E *Ajuga reptans*

Bugle
Bugle rampante
Kriechende Günsel
Consuelda media
Búgula
Bugola
Kruipend zenegroen

F *Sedum rupestre*
Jenny's Stonecrop
Orpin des rochers
Felsen-Fetthenne
Uñas de gato
Borracina rupestre
Tripmadam

G *Thymus*
Thyme
Thym
Thymian
Tomillo
Timo
Tijm

H *Sempervivum montanum*
Mountain houseleek
Joubarbe des montagnes
Berg-Hauswurz
Semprevivo montano
Berghuislook

A *Capsicum annuum*

Pepper

Piment d'ornement

Paprika

Pimiento

Peperone

B *Ocimum basilicum*

Basil

Basilic

Basilikum

Albahaca

Basilico

Basilicum

C *Salvia officinalis*

Common Sage

Sauge officinale

Salbei

Salvia común

Salvia comune

Echte salie

D *Anthriscus cerefolium*

Chervil

Cerfeuil commun

Echter Kerbel

Perifollo

Cerfoglio

Echte kervel

E *Cotinus coggygria*

Smoke Tree

Arbre à perruques

Roter Perückenstrauch

Árbol de las pelucas

Albero della nebbia

Pruikenboom

F *Heuchera*

Alum Root

Heuchère

Purpurglöckchen

Campanillas de coral

Purperklokje

Chelsea Flower
Show, London, UK

Hampton Court Flower Show, London, UK

A *Echeveria montanum*	**B** *Begonia*	**C** *Matteuccia struthiopteris*	**D** *Echeveria*	**E** *Haworthia*	**F** *Aloe*	**G** *Sempervivum*
Hen and Chicks	Bégonia	Ostrich fern	Hen and Chicks	Haworthie	Aloès	Houseleek
Écheveria	Begonie	Fougère allemande	Écheveria		Aloe	Joubarbe
Echeverie		Straußenfarn	Echeverie		Aloë	Hauswurz
Rosa de alabastro		Helecho pluma de avestruz	Rosa de alabastro			Siemprevivas
Echeveria		Felce penna di struzzo				Semprevivo
		Struisvaren				Huislook

D E F G

Hampton Court
Palace Flower
Show, London, UK

A B C D

A *Sedum*
Stonecrop
Orpin
Fetthenne
Hierba callera
Borracina
Vetkruid

B *Aeonium*
Tree Houseleek
Aéonium

C *Echeveria glauca*
Mexican Hen
and Chicks
Écheveria bleue
Echeverie

D *Sempervivum*
Houseleek
Joubarbe
Hauswurz
Siemprevivas
Semprevivo
Huislook

Hampton Court Flower Show, London, UK

A *Erigeron karvinskianus*
Mexican Fleabane
Vergerette de Karvinski
Mexikanisches Berufskraut
Margarita cimarrona
Cespica karvinskiana
Muurfijnstraal

B *Buddleja davidii 'Wisteria Lane'*
Butterfly Bush
Buddleia de David
Schmetterlingsflieder
Arbusto de las mariposas
Buddleia
Vlinderstruik

C *Pilosella aurantiaca*
Fox and Cubs
Épervière orangée
Orangerotes Habichtskraut
Pilosella aurantiaca
Pilosella aurantiaca
Oranje havikskruid

Chelsea Flower Show, London, UK

Chelsea Flower
Show, London, UK

Chelsea Flower
Show, London, UK

Galvanised metal
Métal galvanisé
Verzinktes Metall
Metal galvanizado
Metallo zincato
Gegalvaniseerd metaal

A *Daucus carota subsp. Sativus 'Royal Chantenay'*

Carrot

Carotte

Karotte

Zanahoria

Carota

Wortel

B *Helichrysum italicum*

Curry Plant

Immortelle d'Italie

Zwerg-Currystrauch

Siempreviva del monte

Elicriso italiano

Kerrieplant

C *Thymus*

Thyme

Thym

Thymian

Tomillo

Timo

Tijm

D *Petunia 'Tumbelina'*

Petunia
Pétunia aux fleurs doubles
Petunie

E *Satureja Douglasii*

Yerba Buena
Menthe indienne
Hängeminze
Hierbabuena
Santoreggia
Indische munt

F *Rheum rhabarbarum*

Rhubarb
Rhubarbe des jardins
Rhabarbar
Ruibarbo
Rabarbaro
Rabarber

G *Diascia barberae 'Romeo Red'*

Twinspur
Diascie
Elfensporn
Diascia
Elfenspoor

119

A *Sempervivum*
Houseleek
Joubarbe
Hauswurz
Siemprevivas
Semprevivo
Huislook

B *Echeveria*
Hen and Chicks
Écheveria
Echeverie
Rosa de alabastro

C *Saxifraga × urbium 'Aureopunctata'*
Golden London Pride
Saxifrage au feuillage épais
Porzellanblümchen
Repollo de San Patricio
Steenbreek

D *Sedum spathulifolium 'Purpureum'*
Purple Spoon-Leaved Stonecrop
Orpin spatulé
Spatelblätttrige Fetthenne
Hierba callera
Borracina
Vetkruid

121

A *Helleborus*
Lenten Rose
Hellébore
Christrose
Eléboro
Elleboro
Kerstroos

B *Erica gracilis*
Cape Heath
Bruyère
Glockenheide
Brezo rosa
Dopheide

A *Saxifraga*
Saxifrage
Steinbrech
Sassifraga
Steenbreek

B *Muscari 'Peppermint'*
Grape Hyacinth
Jacinthe à grappes
Traubenhyazinthe
Giacinto a grappolo
Blauw druifje

C *Phlox 'Amazing Grace'*
Flox
Flogo
Vlambloem

D *Scilla siberica*
Siberian Squill
Scille de Sibérie
Sibirische Blaustern
Esquila siberiana
Scilla siberica
Oosterse sterhyacint

A *Equisetum ramosissimum var. japonicum*

Japanese Horsetail
Prêle rameuse japonaise
Ästiger Schachtelhalm
Vertakte paardenstaart

B *Primula bulleyana*

Bulley's Primrose
Primevère candélabre
Etagen-Schlüsselblume
Prímula bulleyana
Primula di Bulley
Sleutelbloem

C *Gunnera manicata*

Chilean rhubarb
Rhubarbe géante
Mammutblatt
Ruibarbo gigante
Rabarbaro gigante
Mammoetblad

D *Juncus effusus f. spiralis*

Corkscrew rush
Jonc spiralé
Flatter-Binse
Junco espiral
Pitrus

E *Ginkgo*

Japanse notenboom

F *Pelargonium peltatum*
Ivy-Leaf Geranium
Géranium-lierre
Efeu-Pelargonie
Gitanilla
Geranio edera
Hanggeranium

G *Argyranthemum*
Marguerite Daisy
Argyranthème
Strauchmargerite
Margarita
Margheritina
Struikmargriet

H *Lysimachia nummularia 'Aurea'*
Golden Creeping Jenny
Lysimaque couvre-sol
Gelbes Pfennigkraut
Planta de la moneda
Lysimachia nummularia
Penningkruid

A *Verbena bonariensis*

Argentinian Vervain

Verveine de
Buenos-Aires

Argentinisches
Eisenkraut

Vervena argentina

Verbena di
Buenos Aires

Stijf ijzerhard

B *Cosmos bipinnatus
'Gazebo Mixed'*

Cosmos

Cosmos bipenné

Schmuckkörbchen

Cosmea

C *Ribes rubrum
'Jonkheer Van Tets'*

Redcurrant

Groseillier à
grappes rouges

Rote Johannisbeere

Grosellero

Ribes rosso

Aalbes

D *Ocimum basilicum*

Sweet Basil

Basilic

Basilikum

Albahaca

Basilico

Basilicum

E *Echeveria*
Hen and Chicks
Écheveria
Echeverie
Rosa de alabastro

F *Begonia*
Bégonia
Begonie

G *Matteuccia struthiopteris*
Ostrich fern
Fougère allemande
Straußenfarn
Helecho pluma de avestruz
Felce penna di struzzo
Struisvaren

A *Viola tricolor*
Heartsease
Pensée sauvage
Wildes Stiefmütterchen
Pensamiento tricolor
Viola del pensiero
Driekleurig viooltje

B *Tulipa*
Tulip
Tulipe
Tulpe
Tulipán
Tulipano
Tulp

C *Cycas revoluta*
Japanese sago palm
Cycas du Japon
Japanischer Sagopalmfarn
Falsa palmera
Cycaspalm

D *Hedera helix*
Ivy
Lierre grimpant
Efeu
Hiedra común
Edera comune
Klimop

E *Cyrtomium falcatum*
Japanese Holly Fern
Fougère-houx
Mond-Sichelfarn
Helecho acebo
Felce agrifoglio
IJzervaren

F *Hosta 'Sum and Substance'*
Plantain Lilly
Hosta
Herzblattlilie
Planta de lidia
Hartlelie

G *Pseudopanax crassifolius*
Lancewood
Speerbaum
Horoeka

London, UK

A *Sanvitalia procumbens*
Creeping Zinnia
Sanvitalie
Husarenknopf
Zinnia rastrera mexicana
Sanvitalia
Huzarenknoop

B *Diascia*
Twinspur
Diascie
Elfensporn
Reina rosada
Elfenspoor

C *Argyranthemum*
Marguerite Daisy
Argyranthème
Strauchmargerite
Margarita
Margheritina
Struikmargriet

D *Petunia*
Pétunia
Petunie

E *Pelargonium*
Geranium
Pélargonium
Pelargonie
Geranio

A *Tagetes patula*

Mexican Marigold

Oeillets d'Inde

Aufrechte
Studentenblume

Damasquina

Tagete comune

Afrikaantje

B *Erigeron
karvinskianus*

Mexican Fleabane

Vergerette de
Karvinski

Mexikanisches
Berufskraut

Margarita cimarrona

Cespica karvinskiana

Muurfijnstraal

C *Solanum
lycopersicum*

Cherry Tomato

Tomate

Kirschtomate

Pomodoro

Tomaat

D *Salvia officinalis*
Common Sage
Sauge officinale
Salbei
Salvia común
Salvia comune
Echte salie

E *Thymus*
Thyme
Thym
Thymian
Tomillo
Timo
Tijm

F *Sempervivum*
Houseleek
Joubarbe
Hauswurz
Siemprevivas
Semprevivo
Huislook

A *Tulipa*
Tulip
Tulipe
Tulpe
Tulipán
Tulipano
Tulp

B *Scilla peruviana*
Portuguese Squill
Scille du Pérou
Peruanische Blaustern
Jacinto azul estrellado
Scilla maggiore

C *Narcissus jonquilla*
Jonquil
Narcisse
Jonquille
Narciso
Narcis

D *Ipheion uniflorum*
Spring Starflower
Iphéion uniflore
Einblütige Frühlingsstern
Ipheion
Ipheion uniflorum
Oude wijfjes

E *Viola*
Pansy
Pensée
Stiefmütterchen
Pensamiento
Viola del pensiero
Viooltje

F *Nigella damascena*
Love-in-the-Mist
Nigelle de Damas
Jungfer-im-Grünen
Arañuela
Fanciullaccia
Juffertje-in-het-groe

137

A *Galanthus nivalis*
Snowdrop
Perce-neige
Schneeglöckchen
Galanto
Bucaneve
Sneeuwklokje

B *Begonia 'Million Kisses'*
Bégonia
Begonie

C *Ginkgo*
Japanse notenboom

D *Erigeron karvinskianus*
Mexican Fleabane
Vergerette de Karvinski
Mexikanisches Berufskraut
Margarita cimarrona
Cespica karvinskiana
Muurfijnstraal

A *Nigella damascena*	**B** *Sempervivum*	**C** *Stipa tenuissima*	**D** *Festuca glauca*
Love-in-the-mist	Houseleek	Mexican feather grass	Blue Fescue
Nigelle de Damas	Joubarbe	Cheveux d'ange	Fétuque bleue
Jungfer-im-Grünen	Hauswurz	Zartes Federgras	Blauschwingel
Abésoda	Siemprevivas	Pluma hierba mexicana	Festuca azulada
Nigella	Semprevivo	Erba piumata del Messico	Festuca azzurra
Juffertje-in-het-groen	Huislook	Mexicaans vedergras	Blauw schapengras

A *Solanum lycopersicum*
   'Tumbling Tom Red'
Tomato
Tomate
Pomodoro
Tomaat

B *Sempervivum*
Houseleek
Joubarbe
Hauswurz
Siemprevivas
Semprevivo
Huislook

C *Aeonium simsii*
Aeonium
Aéonium

A *Lamprocapnos spectabilis*
Bleeding Heart
Cœur de Marie
Tränendes Herz
Lamprocapnos
Cuore di Maria
Gebroken hartje

B *Hesperis matronalis*
Dame's rocket
Julienne des dames
Gewöhnliche Nachtviole
Juliana
Violaciocca antoniana
Damastbloem

C *Viola 'Sorbet Mixed'*
Pansy
Pensée
Stiefmütterchen
Pensamiento
Viola del pensiero
Viooltje

D *Myosotis*
Forget-Me-Not
Myosotis
Vergissmeinnicht
Nomeolvides
Nontiscordardimé
Vergeet-mij-nietje

E *Viola*
Pansy
Pensée
Stiefmütterchen
Pensamiento
Viola del pensiero
Viooltje

F *Fragaria × ananassa*
Strawberry
Fraisié cultivé
Gartenerdbeere
Fresa
Fragola coltivata
Aardbei

A *Sedum*
Stonecrop
Orpin
Fetthenne
Hierba callera
Borracina
Vetkruid

B *Aloe*
Aloès
Aloë

C *Echeveria*
Hen and Chicks
Écheveria
Echeverie
Rosa de alabastro

D *Trachelospermum jasminoides*
Confederate Jasmine
Faux jasmin
Sternjasmin
Jazmín estrella
Falso gelsomino
Sterjasmijn

A *Allium*
Ornamental Onion
Ail d'ornement
Zierlauch
Ajo ornamental
Aglio ornamentale
Sierui

B *Viola tricolor*
Heartsease
Pensée tricolore
Stiefmütterchen
Pensamiento salvaje
Viola del pensiero
Driekleurig viooltje

C *Allium schoenoprasum*
Chives
Ciboulette
Schnittlauch
Cebollino
Erba cipollina
Bieslook

D *Mentha*
Mint
Menthe
Pfefferminze
Menta
Munt

Rusty Metal
Décoration en métal rouillé
Rostige Deko
Metal oxidado
Metallo arrugginito
Roestig metaal

A *Salvia officinalis*
Common Sage
Sauge officinale
Salbei
Salvia común
Salvia comune
Echte salie

B *Origanum vulgare aureum*
Golden Oregano
Origan doré
Goldener Oregano
Orégano común
Origano aureo
Wilde marjolein

C *Lavendula pinnata*
Fernleaf Lavender
Lavande
Kanarischer Lavendel
Matorrisco de Lanzarote
Lavanda
Lavendel

D *Petroselinum*
Parsley
Persil
Petersilie
Perejil
Prezzemolo
Peterselie

E *Rosmarinus officinalis*
Rosemary
Romarin
Rosmarin
Romero
Rosmarino
Rozemarijn

A *Viola tricolor*
Heartsease
Pensée tricolore
Wildes
Stiefmütterchen
Pensamiento salvaje
Viola del pensiero
Driekleurig viooltje

A *Hakonechloa macra 'Aureola'*
Hakone grass
Herbe du Japon
Japan-Zwergschilf
Hierba de Japón
Erba Hakone
Japans berggras

B *Euphorbia × martinii*
Martin's Spurge
Euphorbe
Busch-Wolfsmilch
Euphorbia
Euforbia
Wolfsmelk

C *Hydrangea*
Hortensia
Hortensie
Ortensia

Chelsea Flower Show, London, UK

A *Rosa*
Rose
Rosier
Roos

B *Calibrachoa*
Million Bells
Zauberglöckchen
Petunia calibrachoa
Petunia nana
Minipetunia

C *Lilium*	**D** *Argyranthemum*	**E** *Diascia*	**F** *Digitalis purpurea*	**G** *Zantedeschia elliottiana*	**H** *Salvia pratensis*
Lily	Marguerite Daisy	Twinspur	Foxglove	Calla lily	Meadow Clary
Lys	Argyranthème	Elfensporn	Digitale pourpre	Arum d'Ethiopie	Sauge des prés
Lilie	Strauchmargerite	Elfenspoor	Roter Fingerhut	Zantedeschien	Wiesensalbei
Lirio	Margarita		Dedalera	Cala	Salvia de los prados
Giglio	Margheritina		Digitale rossa	Calla	Salvia dei prati
Lelie	Struikmargriet		Vingerhoedskruid	Aronskelk	Veldsalie

A *Lysimachia vulgaris*
Loosestrife
Lysimaque
Gewöhnlicher
Gilbweiderich
Planta de la moneda
Lysimachia
Wederik

B *Sempervivum*
Houseleek
Joubarbe
Hauswurz
Siemprevivas
Semprevivo
Huislook

C *Sedum*
Stonecrop
Orpin
Fetthenne
Hierba callera
Borracina
Vetkruid

D *Pittosporum*
   tenuifolium
Black Matipo
Pittospore
Schmalblättriger
Klebsame
Azahar de la China
Pittosporo
Australische laurier

E *Echeveria*
Hen and Chicks
Écheveria
Echeverie
Rosa de alabastro

F *Festuca glauca*
Blue Fescue
Fétuque bleue
Blauschwingel
Festuca azulada
Festuca azzurra
Blauw schapengras

163

A *Echeveria*
Hen and Chicks
Écheveria
Echeverie
Rosa de alabastro

B *Sempervivum*
Houseleek
Joubarbe
Hauswurz
Sieprevivas
Semprevivo
Huislook

C *Haworthia*
Haworthie

A *Hedera helix*
Ivy
Lierre grimpant
Efeu
Hiedra común
Edera comune
Klimop

Wood
Bois
Holz
Madera
Legno
Hout

A *Vitis venifera*
Grape Vine
Vigne
Weinrebe
Vid
Vite
Druif

A *Sempervivum
  tectorum*
Common Houseleek
Joubarbe des toits
Dach-Hauswurz
Siempreviva mayor
Semprevivo maggiore
Gewone huislook

B *Sempervivum*
Houseleek
Joubarbe
Hauswurz
Siemprevivas
Semprevivo
Huislook

Athens, Greece

Kent, UK

177

A *Lavandula stoechas*
French Lavender
Lavande papillon
Schopf-Lavendel
Cantueso
Lavanda selvatica
Franse lavendel

B *Salix matsudana 'Tortuosa'*
Twisted Willow
Saule tortueux
Korkenzieher-Weide
Sauce tortuoso
Salice di Pechino
Kronkelwilg

C *Viola tricolor*
Heartsease
Pensée tricolore
Stiefmütterchen
Pensamiento
Viola del pensiero
Viooltje

A *Hydrangea macrophylla*
Hydrangea
Hortensia
Hortensie
Ortensia dei fioristi

B *Lavandula stoechas*
French Lavender
Lavande papillon
Schopf-Lavendel
Cantueso
Lavanda selvatica
Franse lavendel

SEED PACKETS

HERBS vegetables WILD FLOWERS

SEEDLINGS

COMPOST

COMPOST

GREENHOUSE CADDY

GLOVES TWINE

SPUDS

COMPOST

PEELINGS GREENS

A *Pelargonium odoratissimum*
Scented Geranium
Géranium odorant
Duftgeranie
Scented geranium
Geranio odoroso
Rozenpelargonium

B *Pelargonium*
Geranium
Pélargonium
Pelargonie
Geranio

A *Petunia Surfinia 'Deep Red'*
Petunia
Pétunia
Petunie

B *Ageratum houstonianum*
Bluemink
Agératum
Gewöhnlicher Leberbalsam
Damasquino
Mexicaantje

C *Antirrhinum*
Snapdragon
Muflier
Löwenmäulchen
Boca de dragón
Antirrino
Grote leeuwenbek

D *Lobelia 'Trailing Sapphire'*
Lobélie
Lobelie

E *Brachyscome iberidifolia*
Swan River Daisy
Brachycome à feuilles d'Ibaris
Blaues Gänseblümchen
Brachicome
Brascicome
Australisch madeliefje

F *Portulaca*
Rose Moss
Pourpier
Portulak
Portulaca
Postelein

G *Calibrachoa*
Million Bells
Zauberglöckchen
Petunia calibrachoa
Petunia nana
Minipetunia

H *Vinca minor*
Lesser Perinwinkle
Petite pervenche
Kleines Immergrün
Periwinkle pequeño
Pervinca minore
Kleine maagdenpalm

I *Iris reticulata 'Alida'*
Early Bulbous Iris
Iris réticulé
Netzblatt-Schwertlilie
Lirio
Dwergiris

A *Valeriana officinalis*
Valerian
Valériane officinale
Echter Baldrian
Valeriana común
Valeriana comune
Echte valeriaan

B *Persicaria*
Knotweeds
Persicaire
Kleinkopfiger Knöterich
Duizendknoop

C *Astrantia*
Masterwort
Astrance
Sterndolde
Sanicula hembra
Astranzia
Zeeuws knoopje

D *Bupleurum longifolium*
Thoroughwax
Buplèvre à longues feuilles
Langblättriges Hasenohr
Bupleuro con foglie lunghe
Goudscherm

A *Petroselinum*
Parsley
Persil
Petersilie
Perejil
Prezzemolo
Peterselie

B *Rumex sanguineus*
Red-veined Sorrel
Oseille sanguine
Hain-Ampfer
Planta de
Acedera Roja
Romice sanguineo
Bloedzuring

C *Allium schoenoprasum*
Chives
Ciboulette
Schnittlauch
Cebollino
Erba cipollina
Bieslook

D *Mentha × piperita*
Peppermint
Menthe
Pfefferminze
Menta piperita
Munt

E *Solanum lycopersicum*
Tomato
Tomate
Pomodoro
Tomaat

F *Tagetes patula*
Mexican Marigold
Oeillets d'Inde
Aufrechte
Studentenblume
Damasquina
Tagete comune
Afrikaantje

Lancashire, UK

A *Echinacea purpurea*
Purple Coneflower
Rudbeckie pourpre
Purpur-Sonnenhut
Equinacéa purpurea
Echinacea viola
Rode zonnehoed

B *Pelargonium*
Geranium
Pélargonium
Pelargonie
Geranio

C *Rudbeckia hirta*
Black-Eyed Susan
Rudbeckie hérissée
Schwarzäugige
Rudbeckie
Rudbeckia irta
Ruige rudbeckia

D *Lamium maculatum*
Spotted Deadnettle
Lamier maculé
Gefleckte Taubnessel
Ortiga manchada
Falsa ortica macchiata
Gevlekte dovenetel

Sydney, Australia

A *Echeveria*

Hen and Chicks
Écheveria
Echeverie
Rosa de alabastro

B *Sedum*

Stonecrop
Orpin
Fetthenne
Hierba callera
Borracina
Vetkruid

C *Euphorbia characias subsp. Wulfenii*

Mediterranean spurge
Euphorbe des vallons wulfenii
Palisaden-Wolfsmilch
Euforbio mediterráneo
Euphorbia characias
Wolfsmelk

D *Kniphofia uvaria 'Nobilis'*

Red Hot Poker
Tritome à longues grappes
Schopf-Fackellilie
Vuurpijl

Sydney, Australia

Dorset, UK

Glass
Verre
Glas
Vidrio
Vetro

A *Lamium maculatum*
Spotted Deadnettle
Lamier maculé
Gefleckte Taubnessel
Ortiga manchada
Falsa ortica macchiata
Gevlekte dovenetel

B *Campanula*
Bellflower
Campanule
Glockenblume
Klokjesbloem

C *Petunia*
Pétunia
Petunie

Hampshire, UK

A *Solenostemon*
'Kong Series'

Coleus

Coléus

Buntnessel

Cóleos

Coleus

Siernetel

A *Geranium*
Cranesbill
Géranium
Storchschnabel
Geranio
Ooievaarsbek

B *Phormium*
New Zealand Flax
Lin de Nouvelle-Zélande
Neuseelandflachs
Lino de Nueva Zelanda
Lino della Nuova Zelanda
Nieuw-Zeelands vlas

C *Heuchera*
Alum Root
Heuchère
Purpurglöckchen
Campanilla de coral
Purperklokje

D *Sedum*	**E** *Thymus*	**F** *Salvia*	**G** *Lychnis flos-cuculi*
Stonecrop	Thyme	Sage	Ragged Robin
Orpin	Thym	Sauge	Lychnis fleur de coucou
Fetthenne	Thymian	Salbei	Kuckucks-Lichtnelke
Hierba callera	Tomillo	Salvia	Flor de cuclillo
Borracina	Timo	Salvia	Fior di cuculo cuculi
Vetkruid	Tijm	Salie	Echte koekoeksbloem

Hampshire, UK

Devon, UK

A *Pulmonaria*
Lungwort
Pulmonaire
Lungenkraut
Hoja del pulmón
Longkruid

B *Leucojum vernum*
Spring Snowflake
Nivéole de printemps
Märzenbecher
Campanilla de verano
Campanellino
Lenteklokje

C *Cyclamen coum*
Eastern Cyclamen
Cyclamen de Cos
Vorfrühlings-
Alpenveilchen
Ciclamino dei boschi
Cyclaam van Coa

D *Helleborus*
Lenten Rose
Hellébore
Christrose
Eléboro
Elleboro
Kerstroos

E *Galanthus nivalis*
Snowdrop
Perce-neige
Schneeglöckchen
Galanto
Bucaneve
Sneeuwklokje

F *Ribes alpinum*
Mountain Currant
Groseillier des Alpes
Alpen-Johannisbeere
Grosellero de
los Alpes
Ribes rosso
Alpenbes

G *Prunus*
Cherry
Cerisier
Kirsche
Prunus
Ciliegio
Kers

H *Muscari*
Grape Hyacinth
Jacinthe à grappes
Traubenhyazinthe
Giacinto a grappolo
Blauw druifje

I *Primula*
Primrose
Primevère
Primel
Primula
Sleutelbloem

J *Anemone blanda*
Blue-Flowered
Winter Windflower
Anémone de Grèce
Balkan-Windröschen
Anémona azul
Oosterse anemoon

Hampshire, UK

A *Lilium hybridum 'African Queen'*
Lily
Lys trompette jaune
Trompetenlilie
Lirio
Giglio
Lelie

B *Verbena hastata*
American Vervain
Verveine hastée
Lanzen-Eisenkraut
Verbena azul americana
Verbena blu
Ijzerhard

C *Hydrangea*
Hortensia
Hortensie
Ortensia

D *Ilex aquifolium*
Common Holly
Houx
Europäische Stechpalme
Acebo
Agrifoglio
Hulst

E *Trachycarpus fortunei*
Chinese Windmill Palm
Palmier de Chine
Chinesische Hanfpalme
Palmera excelsa
Palma cinese
Henneppalm

F *Dicksonia antarctica*
Soft Tree Fern
Fougère arborescente
Australischer Taschenfarn
Helecho arbóreo
Felce arborea
Tasmaanse boomvaren

A *Calibrachoa*
Million Bells
Zauberglöckchen
Petunia calibrachoa
Petunia nana
Minipetunia

B *Muehlenbeckia*
Maidenhair
Drahtstrauch
Enredadera de
alambre

C *Sanvitalia
procumbens*
Creeping Zinnia
Sanvitalie rampante
Husarenknopf
Ojo de gallo
Sanvitalia
Huzarenknoop

D *Petunia*
Pétunia
Petunie

E *Bacopa monnieri*
Water Hyssop
Hysope d'eau
Kleines Fettblatt
Hisopo de agua
Bacopa

A *Fritillaria meleagris*
Snake's Head Fritillary
Fritillaire pintade
Schachblume
Tablero de damas
Fritillaria testa
di serpente
Kievitsbloem

East Sussex, UK

Clematis:
A 'Alba Luxurians'
B 'Madame Julia
   Correvan'
C 'Little Nell'
D 'Blue Angel'
E 'Mary Rose'
F 'Royal Velours'
G 'Madame Julia
   Correvan'
Clématite
Waldrebe
Clemátide
Clematide
Bosrank

Terracotta
Terre cuite
Terrakotta
Tierra cocida

A *Helianthus annuus 'Waooh'*
Sunflower
Tournesol
Sonnenblume
Girasol
Girasole comune
Zonnebloem

Cambridgeshire, UK

Hampton Court Flower Show, London, UK

A *Sedum spathulifolium 'Purpureum'*

Purple Spoon-Leaved Stonecrop

Orpin spatulé

Spatelblätttrige Fetthenne

Sedum

Borracina cappa bianca

Vetkruid

B *Sempervivum*

Houseleek

Joubarbe

Hauswurz

Siemprevivas

Semprevivo

Huislook

234

A *Echeveria*
Hen and Chicks
Écheveria
Echeverie
Rosa de alabastro

B *Sempervivum*
Houseleek
Joubarbe
Hauswurz
Siemprevivas
Semprevivo
Huislook

C *Sedum*
Stonecrop
Orpin
Fetthenne
Hierba callera
Borracina
Vetkruid

D *Sedum spathulifolium 'Cappa Blanca'*
Purple Spoon-Leaved Stonecrop
Orpin spatulé 'Cappa Blanca'
Spatelblätttrige Fetthenne
Sedum
Borracina cappa bianca
Vetkruid

E *Mentha*
Mint
Menthe
Minze
Menta
Munt

A *Papaver somniferum*

Opium Poppy
Pavot somnifère
Schlafmohn
Adormidera
Papavero da oppio
Slaapbol

B *Convolvulus sabatius*

Blue Rock Bindweed
Liseron de Mauritanie
Blaue Mauritius
Campanilla azul
Convolvolo di Vado Ligure
Winde

C *Erigeron karvinskianus*

Mexican Fleabane
Vergerette de Karvinski
Mexikanisches Berufskraut
Margarita cimarrona
Cespica karvinskiana
Muurfijnstraal

D *Laurus nobilis*

Lorbeer
Laurier vrai
Echter Lorbeer
Laurel
Alloro
Laurier

E *Lobelia erinus*

Garden Lobelia
Lobélie érine
Männertreu
lobelia azul
Fiore cardinale
Lobelia

F *Berberis*

Barberry
Epine-vinette
Berberitze
Agracejo rojo
Crespin
Zuurbes

Kebun Raya, Bogor,
Indonesia

A *Cerinthe major 'Purpurascens'*
Honeywort
Grande cérinthe
Große Wachsblume
Ceriflor púrpura
Erba vajola
Grote wasbloem

B *Cotinus coggygria 'Royal Purple'*
Smokebush
Arbre à perruques
Roter Perückenstrauch
Árbol de las pelucas
Albero della nebbia
Pruikenboom

C *Hakonechloa macra 'Aureola'*
Hakone grass
Herbe du Japon
Japan-Zwergschilf
Hierba de Japón
Erba Hakone
Japans berggras

D *Rosmarinus officinalis*
Rosemary
Romarin
Rosmarin
Romero
Rosmarino
Rozemarijn

Wheels
Roues
Räder
Ruedas
Ruote
Wielen

Berkshire, UK

Chelsea Flower Show, London, UK

A *Lythrum salicaria*
Purple Loosestrife
Salicaire commune
Gewöhnlicher
Blutweiderich
Salicaris
Salcerella
Grote kattenstaart

B *Polystichum polyblepharum*
Japanese Lace Fern
Aspidie du Japon
Japanischer
Schildfarn
Helecho de escudo
Felce setifera
Glansschildvaren

C *Vitis vinifera*
Grape Vine
Vigne
Weinrebe
Vid
Vite comune
Druif

D *Helenium 'Wyndley'*
Sneezeweed
Hélénie
Sonnenbraut
Chapuz
Helenio
Zonnekruid

246

A *Camassia*

Camas
Prärielilie
Prairielelie

B *Carex testacea*

Orange New
Zealand Sedge
Laîche orange
Neuseeland-
Segge
Carex
Carice
Oranjezegge

C *Polemonium
'Heaven Scent'*

Jacob's Ladder
Polémoine
Jakobsleiter
Polemonio
Jacobsladder

D *Cirsium vulgare*

Plume Thistle
Cirse commun
Gewöhnliche
Kratzdistel
Cardillo
Cardo asinino
Vederdistel

E *Polystichum
polyblepharum*

Japanese
Lace Fern
Aspidie du Japon
Japanischer
Schildfarn
Helecho de
escudo
Felce setifera
Glansschildvaren

F *Stipa tenuissima*

Mexican
Feather Grass
Cheveux d'ange
Zartes Federgras
Pluma hierba
mexicana
Erba piumata
del Messico
Mexicaans
vedergras

Berkshire, UK

A *Artemisia*
Wormwood
Armoise
Wermut
Artemisa
Alsem

B *Salvia hormium*
Clary Sage
Sauge verte
Schopf-Salbei
Salvia viridis
Salvia annuale
Bonte salie

C *Lactuca*
Lettuce
Laitue
Gartensalat
Lechuga
Lactuca
Sla

D *Linum perenne*
Bue Flax
Lin vivace
Stauden-Lein
Lino perenne
Lino di Siberia
Vlas

E *Calendula officinalis*
Marigold
Souci officinal
Ringelblume
Caléndula
Calendula officinale
Goudsbloem

F *Petroselinum*
Parsley
Persil
Petersilie
Perejil
Prezzemolo
Peterselie

G *Perilla frutescens*
Perilla
Pérille
Basilico cinese
Shiso

H *Viola*
Pansy
Pensée
Stiefmütterchen
Pensamiento
Viola del pensiero
Viooltje

I *Polystichum polyblepharum*

Japanese Lace Fern

Aspidie du Japon

Japanischer Schildfarn

Helecho de escudo

Felce setifera

Glansschildvaren

J *Stipa tenuissima*

Mexican Feather Grass

Cheveux d'ange

Zartes Federgras

Pluma hierba mexicana

Erba piumata del Messico

Mexicaans vedergras

K *Polemonium 'Heaven Scent'*

Jacob's Ladder

Polémoine

Jakobsleiter

Polemonio

Jacobsladder

A *Cucurbita*
Squash
Courge
Kürbis
Calabaza
Zucca
Pompoen

255

Mirrors
Miroirs
Spiegel
Espejos
Specchi
Spiegels

Quebec, Canada

Hertfordshire, UK

A *Lonicera japonica*

Japanese
Honeysuckle

Chèvrefeuille
du Japon

Japanisches
Geißblatt

Madreselva

Caprifoglio
giapponese

Japanse
kamperfoelie

B *Phyllostachys nigra*

Black Bamboo

Bambou noir

Schwarzrohrbambus

Bambú negro

Bambù nero

Zwarte bamboe

C *Campanula*
  portenschlagiana

Wall Bellflower

Campanule des
murailles

Polsterglockenblume

Campanula

Klokjesbloem

D *Hedera helix*
Ivy
Lierre grimpant
Efeu
Hiedra común
Edera comune
Klimop

E *Salvia nemorosa*
Balkan clary
Sauge des bois
Hain-Salbei
Salvia de bosque
Salvia
Bossalie

Kent, UK

Berkeley,
California, USA

London, UK

Berkshire, UK

A *Hedera helix*

Ivy

Lierre grimpant

Efeu

Hiedra común

Edera comune

Klimop

B *Salvia officinalis
'Icterina'*

Golden Garden Sage

Sauge officinale
panachée

Buntblättriger Salbei

Salvia común

Salvia comune

Echte salie

C *Acer palmatum*

Japanese Maple

Érable palmé

Fächerahorn

Arce japonés
palmeado

Acero palmato

Japanse esdoorn

D *Cosmos*
Schmuckkörbchen
Cosmea

E *Hedera helix*
Ivy
Lierre grimpant
Efeu
Hiedra común
Edera comune
Klimop

F *Salvia nemorosa*
'Caradonna'
Balkan clary
Sauge des bois
Hain-Salbei
Salvia de bosque
Salvia
Bossalie

G *Verbena bonariensis*
'Lollipop'
Argentinian Vervain
Verveine de
Buenos-Aires
Argentinisches
Eisenkraut
Verbena púrpura
Verbena di
Buenos Aires
IJzerhard

H *Echinacea purpurea*
'White Swan'
Purple Coneflower
Rudbeckie pourpre
Purpur-Sonnenhut
Equinacéa purpurea
Echinacea viola
Rode zonnehoed

I *Rosa 'Iceberg'*
Rose
Rosier à fleur
groupées
Roos

Sydney, Australia

Tin cans
Boîtes en fer-blanc
Blechdosen
Latas de estaño
Barattoli di latta
Blikjes

Chelsea Flower
Show, London, UK

A *Scilla siberica*
Siberian Squill
Scille de Sibérie
Sibirischer Blaustern
Esquila siberiana
Falso giacinto
Oosterse sterhyacint

B *Muscari*
Grape Hyacinth
Jacinthe à grappes
Traubenhyazinthe
Violeta
Giacinto a grappolo
Blauw druifje

C *Muehlenbeckia*
Maidenhair
Drahtstrauch

D *Viola*
Pansy
Pensée
Stiefmütterchen
Pensamiento
Viola del pensiero
Viooltje

A *Convolvulus sabatius*
Blue Rock Bindweed
Liseron de Mauritanie
Blaue Mauritius
Campanilla azul
Convolvoli
Winde

B *Pelargonium*
Geranium
Pélargonium
Pelargonie
Geranio

C *Verbena × hybrida*
Vervain
Verveine
Hängeverbene
Verbena
IJzerhard

D *Calibrachoa*
Million Bells
Zauberglöckchen
Petunia calibrachoa
Petunia nana
Minipetunia

E *Lobelia erinus*
Trailing Lobelia
Lobélie érine
Männertreu
Lobelia erinus
Fiore cardinale
Tuinlobelia

Chaumont sur
Loire, France

A *Solanum lycopersicum* 'Tumbling Tom Red'
Tomato
Tomate
Pomodoro
Tomaat

284

B *Lactuca sativa*
Lettuce
Laitue cultivée
Pflücksalat
Lechuga
Lattuga
Sla

A *Lythrum salicaria*
Purple Loose Strife
Salicaire
Gewöhnlicher Blutweiderich
Salicaria menor
Salcerella
Kattenstaart

B *Tropaeolum*
Nasturtium
Capucine des jardins
Kapuzinerkresse
Capuchina
Nasturzio
Oost-Indische kers

C *Fragaria*
Strawberry
Fraisier
Garten-Erdbeere
Fresa
Fragaria
Aardbei

A *Anthriscus sylvestris*
Cow Parsley
Cerfeuil sauvage
Wiesen-Kerbel
Perifollo verde
Cerfoglio dei prati
Fluitenkruid

B *Tanacetum parthenium*
Feverfew
Grande camomille
Mutterkraut
Ajenjo del campo
Partenio
Moederkruid

C *Centaurea cyanus*
Cornflower
Bleuet des champs
Kornblume
Aciano
Fiordaliso
Korenbloem

D *Verbena* × *hybrida*
Vervain
Verveine
Hängeverbene
Verbena
IJzerhard

289

A *Viola 'Ruby & Gold'*
Pansy
Pensée
Stiefmütterchen
Pensamiento
Viola del pensiero
Viooltje

A *Helianthus annus*	**B** *Phacelia*	**C** *Papaver somniferum*	**D** *Calendula officinalis*	**E** *Nigella damascena*
Sunflower	Fiddleneck	Opium Poppy	Common Marigold	Love-in-a-Mist
Tournesol	Phacélie à feuilles de tanaisie	Pavot somnifière	Souci officinal	Nigelle de Damas
Sonnenblume	Bienenweide	Schlafmohn	Ringelblume	Jungfer im Grünen
Girasol	Facelia	Adormidera	Caléndula	Falso comino
Girasole	Bijenvoer	Papavero da oppio	Calendula	Fanciullaccia
Zonnebloem		Slaapbol	Goudsbloem	Juffertje-in-het-groen

A *Narcissus*

Daffodil
Narcisse
Narzisse
Narciso
Narcis

B *Hyacinthus*

Hyacinth
Jacinthe véritable
Hyazinthe
Jacinto
Giacinto
Hyacint

C *Crocus chrysanthus
var. fuscotinctus*

Golden Crocus
Crocus botanique jaune
d'or strié de brun
Balkan-Krokus
Crocus
Krokus

Cambodia

A *Lactuca sativa
'Lollo Rosso'*

Lettuce

Laitue cultivée

Gartensalat

Lechuga

Lattuga

Sla

B *Lobelia erinus*
Trailing Lobelia
Lobélie érine
Männertreu
Lobelia azul
Fiore cardinale
Tuinlobelia

A *Mentha × piperita f. citrata 'Basil'*

Basil Mint

Menthe basilic

Basilikumminze

Menta

Munt

B *Primula elatior*
 'Gold Lace'
Oxlip
Primevère élevée
Goldrandprimeln
Flor de las neveras
Primula maggiore
Slanke Sleutelbloem

C *Hyacinthus*
Hyacinth
Jacinthe
Hyazinthe
Jacinto
Giacinto
Hyacint

D *Narcissus*
Miniture Daffodil
Narcisse miniature
Zwergnarzisse
Narciso enano
Narciso nano
Mininarcis

E *Muscari*
Grape Hyacinth
Jacinthe à grappes
Traubenhyazinthe
Giacinto a grappolo
Blauw druifje

Chelsea Flower
Show, London, UK

Chelsea Flower
Show, London, UK

A *Anchusa azurea 'Loddon Royalist'*
Italian bugloss
Buglosse d'Italie
Italienische Ochsenzunge
Lengua de buey
Buglossa
Ossetong

B *Calendula officinalis*
Marigold
Souci officinal
Ringelblume
Caléndula
Calendula officinale
Goudsbloem

C *Salvia officinalis 'Purpurascens'*
Sage
Sauge officinale
Salbei
Salvia
Salie

D *Allium schoenoprasum*
Chives
Ciboulette
Schnittlauch
Cebollino
Erba cipollina
Bieslook

E *Thymus*
Thyme
Thym
Thymian
Tomillo
Timo
Tijm

Tools
Outils
Werkzeuge
Herramientas
Attrezzi
Gereedschap

Hertfordshire, UK

Dorset, UK

Staffordshire, UK

West Midlands, UK

A *Hedera helix*
Ivy
Lierre grimpant
Efeu
Hiedra común
Edera comune
Klimop

A *Hydrangea petiolaris*	**B** *Erysimum hybride 'Bowles Mauve'*	**C** *Viola*	**D** *Heuchera*	**E** *Sempervivum*
Climbing Hydrangea	Wallflower	Pansy	Alum Root	Houseleek
Hortensia grimpant	Giroflée arbustive	Pensée	Heuchère	Joubarbe
Kletter-Hortensie	Violetter Schröterich	Stiefmütterchen	Purpurglöckchen	Hauswurz
Hortensia trepadora	Erysimum	Pensamiento	Campanillas de coral	Siemprevivas
Ortensia petiolaris	Muurbloem	Viola del pensiero	Purperklokje	Semprevivo
Hortensia		Viooltje		Huislook

Warrington, UK

A *Equisetum*
Horsetail
Prêle
Schachtelhalm
Cola de caballo
Equiseto
Paardenstaart

B *Hydrangea macrophylla*
Hydrangea
Hortensia
Hortensie
Ortensia dei fioristi

C *Rosa*
Rose
Rosier
Roos

D *Nepeta*
Catmint
Népète
Katzenminze
Gatera
Gattaia
Kattenkruid

E *Penstemon*
Beardtongues
Penstémon
Bartfaden
Schildpadbloem

F *Geranium*
Cranesbill
Géranium
Storchschnabel
Geranio
Ooievaarsbek

G *Prunus subhirtella*
'Autumnalis Rosea'
Pink Winter Cherry Tree
Cerisier à fleurs
d'automne
Higan-Kirsche
Cerezo
Ciliegio
Sierkers

Shropshire, UK

Worcestershire, UK

A *Primula auricula*
Auricula
Oreille d'ours
Aurikel
Primula auricula
Primula orecchia d'orso
Aurikel

B *Sempervivum*
Houseleek
Joubarbe
Hauswurz
Siemprevivas
Semprevivo
Huislook

C *Sempervivum*
Flowering Houseleek
Floraison de Joubarbe
Blühender Hauswurz
Siemprevias en floración
Semprevivo in fiore
Bloeiende huislook

329

Vintage Garden Roller
Rouleau de jardin ancien
Antike Gartenwalze
Rodillo antiguo de jardín
Antico rullo da giardino
Ouderwetse tuinroller

Worcestershire, UK

A *Geranium macrorrhizum*

Bulgarian Geranium

Géranium à grosses racines

Balkan-Storchschnabel

Geranio

Geranio odoroso

Rotsooievaarsbek

B
Mangle
Mangel
Plancha
Mangano

A *Pinus*

Pine
Pin
Kiefer
Pinos
Pino
Den

B *Carex comans 'Bronze leaved'*

Bronze New Zealand Hair Sedge
Laîche de Nouvelle-Zélande
Schopf-Segge
Carex hoja de bronce
Carice della Nuova Zelanda
Bronsbladige zegge

C *Polystichum*

Fern
Fougère
Schildfarn
Helecho
Felce
Glansschildvaren

D *Asarum europaeum*

European Wild Ginger
Asaret d'Europe
Gewöhnliche Haselwurz
Asarabacara
Asarabacca
Mansoor

E *Hosta*

Plantain Lilly
Herzblattlilie
Planta de lidia
Hartlelie

Middlesex, UK

A *Rosa*
Rose
Rosier
Roos

B *Rosa canina*
Rose hips
Rosier des chiens
Hagebutten
Escaramujo
Cinorrodo
Rozenbottel

C *Pyracantha*
Firethorn Berries
Buisson ardent
Feuerdornfrüchte
Espinos de fuego
Piracanta
Vuurdoorn

D *Crataegus*
Hawthorn Berries
Aubépine
Weißdornfrüchte
Bayas de Crataegus
Bacche di Biancospino
Meidoornbessen

Household Items
Objets du foyer
Haushaltsgegenstände
Artículos para el hogar
Articoli per la casa
Huishoudelijke artikelen

London, UK

A *Buxus sempervirens*
Common box
Buis
Buchsbaum
Boj común
Bosso comune
Buksboom

B *Sempervivum*
Houseleek
Joubarbe
Hauswurz
Siemprevivas
Semprevivo
Huislook

C *Hedera helix*
Ivy
Lierre grimpant
Efeu
Hiedra común
Edera comune
Klimop

D *Polystichum*
Fern
Fougère
Schildfarn
Helecho
Felce
Glansschildvaren

West Midlands, UK

Middlesex, UK

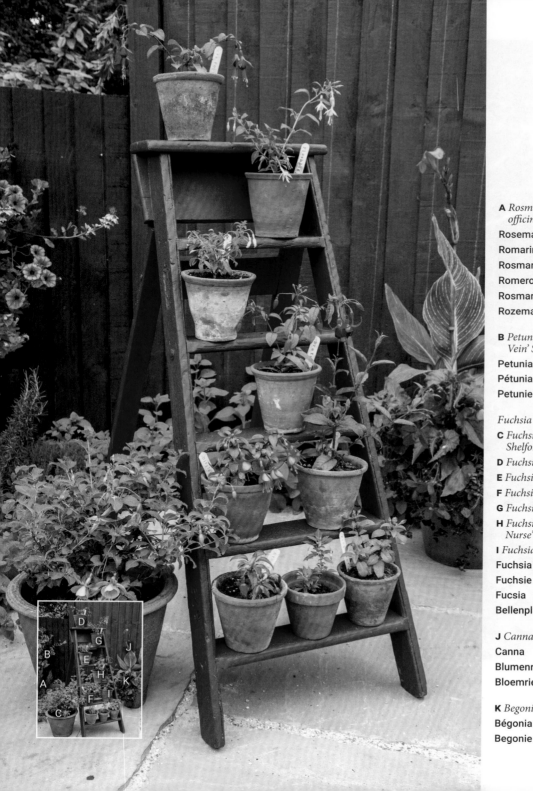

A *Rosmarinus officinalis*
Rosemary
Romarin
Rosmarin
Romero
Rosmarino
Rozemarijn

B *Petunia 'Pink Vein' Surfinia*
Petunia
Pétunia
Petunie

Fuchsia
C *Fuchsia 'Upright Shelford'*
D *Fuchsia 'Popple'*
E *Fuchsia 'Hawkshead'*
F *Fuchsia 'Display'*
G *Fuchsia 'Flashlight'*
H *Fuchsia 'Army Nurse'*
I *Fuchsia 'Riccartonii'*
Fuchsia
Fuchsie
Fucsia
Bellenplant

J *Canna striata*
Canna
Blumenrohr
Bloemriet

K *Begonia*
Bégonia
Begonie

L *Echeveria*
Hen and Chicks
Écheveria
Echeverie
Rosa de alabastro

M *Euphorbia characias*
Mediterranean
Spurge
Euphorbe des
garrigues
Palisaden-Wolfsmilch
Euforbio
mediterráneo
Wolfsmelk

N *Sempervivum*
Houseleek
Joubarbe
Hauswurz
Siemprevivas
Semprevivo
Huislook

Washington, USA

A *Rosmarinus officinalis*
Rosemary
Romarin
Rosmarin
Romero
Rosmarino
Rozemarijn

B *Salvia officinalis*
Common Sage
Sauge officinale
Salbei
Salvia común
Salvia comune
Echte salie

C *Argyranthemum*
Marguerite Daisy
Argyranthème
Strauchmargerite
Margarita
Margheritina
Struikmargriet

D *Campanula*
Bellflower
Campanule
Glockenblume
Campanilla
Campanula
Klokjesbloem

THE KITCHEN GARDEN

Malvern Spring
Festival, UK

Keukenhof Gardens,
Amsterdam,
Netherlands

A *Cornus alba*
White Dogwood
Cornouiller
Weißer Hartriegel
Cornejo siberiano
Corniolo bianco
Witte kornoelje

B *Sempervivum*
Houseleek
Joubarbe
Hauswurz
Siemprevivas
Semprevivo
Huislook

C *Saxifraga*
Saxifrage
Saxifrage
Steinbrech
Saxifraga
Sassifraga
Steenbreek

Chelsea Flower
Show, London, UK

London, UK

A *Sedum*
Stonecrop
Orpin
Fetthenne
Hierba callera
Borracina
Vetkruid

B *Tropaeolum*
Nasturtium
Capucine
Kapuzinerkresse
Capuchina
Nasturzio
Oost-Indische kers

C *Armeria maritima*
Thrift
Armérie maritime
Strand-Grasnelke
Clavelina de mar
Engels gras

A *Echinacea purpurea*
Purple Coneflower
Rudbeckia pourpre
Purpur-Sonnenhut
Equinácea purpurea
Echinacea viola
Rode zonnehoed

B *Trifolium*
Clover
Trèfle
Klee
Trébol
Trifoglio
Klaver

C *Helianthus microcephalus*
Small Woodland Sunflower
Hélianthe
Kleinköpfige Stauden-Sonneblume
Girasol perenne
Elianto
Zonnebloem

D *Oreganum vulgare*
Origanum vulgare
Oregano
Origan
Orégano
Origano
Wilde marjolein

E *Lavandula*
Lavender
Lavande
Lavendel
Lavanda

Liverpool, UK

A

B

C

D

A *Pelargonium*
Geranium
Pélargonium
Pelargonie
Geranio

B *Viola*
Pansy
Penseé
Stiefmütterchen
Pensamiento
Viola del pensiero
Viooltje

C *Diascia*
Twinspur
Diascie
Elfensporn
Elfenspoor

D *Rosmarinus*
  officinalis
Rosemary
Romarin
Rosmarin
Romero
Rosmarino
Rozemarijn

A *Lychnis flos-cuculi*
White Ragged Robin
Lychnis fleur
de coucou
Kuckucks-Lichtnelke
Lychnis
Licnide
Koekoeksbloem

B *Centranthus ruber*
Red Valerian
Centranthe rouge
Rote Spornblume
Milamores
Valeriana rossa
Spoorbloem

C *Salvia officinalis*
Common Sage
Sauge officinale
Salbei
Salvia común
Salvia comune
Echte salie

D *Meconopsis cambrica*
Welsh Poppy
Pavot du Pays
de Galles
Wald-Scheinmohn
Amapola amarila
Papavero del Galles
Schijnpapaver

E *Ocimum basilicum*
Basil
Basilic
Basilikum
Albahaca
Basilico
Basilicum

F *Pelargonium*
Geranium
Pélargonium
Pelargonie
Geranio

G *Impatiens walleriana*
Busy Lizzie
Impatiente
Fleißiges Lieschen
Impaciencia
Balsamina
Vlijtig liesje

H *Hedera helix*
Ivy
Lierre grimpant
Efeu
Hiedra común
Edera comune
Klimop

I *Hydrangea petiolaris*
Climbing Hydrangea
Hortensia grimpant
Kletter-Hortensie
Hortensia trepadora
Ortensia petiolaris
Hortensia

J *Meconopsis cambrica*
Welsh Poppy
Pavot du Pays de Galles
Wald-Scheinmohn
Amapola amarila
Papavero del Galles
Schijnpapaver

K *Euphorbia hypericifolia 'Diamond Frost'*
Baby's Breath Euphorbia
Euphorbe
Zauberschnee
Hierba de la golondrina
Euphorbia
Wolfsmelk

Oxfordshire, UK

A *Ficus carica*
Common Fig
Figuier
Echte Feige
Higuera
Fico
Vijgenboom

New York, USA

Unusual containers
Contenants insolites
Ungewöhnliche Behälter
Contenedores extraordinarios
Contenitori insoliti
Ongebruikelijke potten en bakken

A *Petunia*
Pétunia
Petunie

B *Solanum lycopersimum*
Tomato
Tomate
Pomodoro
Tomaat

C *Nigella damascena*
Love-in-the-mist
Nigelle
Jungfer-im-Grünen
Abésoda
Nigella
Juffertje-in-het-groen

D *Sempervivum*
Houseleek
Joubarbe
Hauswurz
Siemprevias
Semprevivo
Huislook

A *Adiantum pedatum*
Maidenhair Fern
Adiante du Canada
Pfauenrad-
Frauenhaarfarn
Culantrillo de Canadá
Felce adianto
canadese
Hoefijzervaren

B *Soleirolia soleirolii*
Mind-your-own-
business
Helxine
Bubikopf
Lágrimas de ángel
Helxine
Slaapkamergeluk

379

A *Veronicastrum virginicum 'Rosey'*

Culver's root

Véronique

Kandelaber-
Ehrenpreis

Veronicastrum

Radice di Culver

Ereprijs

B *Salvia nemorosa*
Balkan Clary
Sauge des bois
Hain-Salbei
Salvia del bosque
Bossalie

Delphinium
C *'Guardian Lavender'*
D *'Guardian White'*
Larkspur
Dauphinelle
Rittersporn
Espuela de
caballero
Delfinio
Ridderspoor

E *Euonymus japonicus*
Spindle
Fusain du Japon
Kleinblättrige
Japanspindel/
Spindelstrauch
Huso japonés
Evonimo giapponese
Japanse
kardinaalsmuts

A *Scaevola aemula
'Zig Zag'*
Fairy Fan-Flower
Fleur éventail de fée
Blaue Fächerblume
Flor de abanico
Scevola
Waaierbloem

B *Tropaeolum majus*
Garden Nasturtium
Grande Capucine
Kapuzinerkresse
Capuchina
Nasturzio comune
Oost-Indische kers

C *Zea mays*
Sweetcorn
Maïs
Mais
Maíz

D *Lactuca sativa*
Lettuce
Laitue cultivée
Gartensalat
Lechuga
Lattuga
Sla

E *Allium cepa*
Onion
Oignon
Zwiebel
Cebolla
Cipolla
Ui

A *Viola*
Pansy
Pensée
Stiefmütterchen
Pensamiento
Viola del pensiero
Viooltje

B *Tropaeolum*

Nasturtium
Capucine
Kapuzinerkresse
Capuchina
Nasturzio
Oost-Indische
kers

C *Tropaeolum majus*

Garden
nasturtium
Grande capucine
Kapuzinerkresse
Capuchina
Nasturzio
comune
Oost-Indische
kers

D *Phaseolus vulgaris*

French Beans
Haricot commun
Gartenbohne
Judía verde
Fagiolo
Sperziebonen

E *Lactuca sativa 'Dazzle'*

Lettuce
Laitue cultivée
Gartensalat
Lechuga
Lattuga
Sla

F *Lactuca sativa 'Little gem pearl'*

Lettuce
Laitue cultivée
Gartensalat
Lechuga
Lattuga
Sla

G *Cucurbita*

Pumpkin
Potimarron
Kürbis
Pompoen

A *Foeniculum vulgare*
Fennel
Fenouil commun
Fenchel
Hinojo
Finocchio
Venkel

B *Crocosmia*
Montbretia
Montbretie
Montbretia

C *Melissa officinalis*
'Aurea'
Variegated
Lemon Balm
Mélisse citronelle
Zitronenmelisse
Toronjil
Melissa vera
Citroenmelisse

D *Thymus pulegioides*
'Archer's Gold'
Broad-leaved Thyme
Thym faux pouliot
Breitblättriger
Thymian
Tomillo
Timo
Tijm

E *Helichrysum*
italicum
Curry Plant
Immortelle d'Italie
Currykraut
Pluma del príncipe
Elicriso italiano
Kerrieplant

F *Salvia officinalis*
Common Sage
Sauge officinale
Salbei
Salvia común
Salvia comune
Echte salie

A *Petunia*
Pétunia
Petunie

B *Lobelia*
Lobélie
Lobelie

A *Centranthus ruber*
Red Valerian
Centranthe rouge
Rote Spornblume
Milamores
Valeriana rossa
Spoorbloem

B *Mentha*
Mint
Menthe
Minze
Menta
Munt

C *Silene acaulis
'Mount Snowdon'*
Moss Campion
Silène acaule
Polsternelke
Silene musgo
Stengelloze silene

D *Pelargonium*
Geranium
Pélargonium
Pelargonie
Geranio

E *Muscari*
Grape Hyacinth
Jacinthe à grappes
Traubenhyazinthe
Muscari
Giacinto a grappolo
Blauw druifje

F *Narcissus*
Daffodil
Narcisse
Narzisse
Narciso
Narcis

G *Tulipa*
Tulip
Tulipes
Tulpe
Tulipán
Tulipano
Tulp

Hampton Court Flower Show, London, UK

A *Lonicera nitida*

Wilson's Honeysuckle

Chèvrefeuille arbustif

Heckenkirsche

Bontbladige Chinese kamperfoelie

B *Muscari 'Valerie Finnis'*

Grape Hyacinth

Jacinthe à grappes

Traubenhyazinthe

Muscari

Giacinto a grappolo

Blauw druifje

C *Chionodoxa luciliae*

Lucile's glory-of-the-snow

Gloire des neiges

Schneeglanz

Gloria de las nieves

Chionodoxa luciliae

Sneeuwroem

D *Hyacinthus orientalis 'Woodstock'*

Hyacinth

Jacinthe d'orient

Gartenhyazinthe

Jacinto común

Giacinto orientale

Hyacint

E *Narcissus 'Rip Van Winkle'*

Daffodil

Narcisse

Narzisse

Narciso

Narcis

F *Fragaria vesca*
Wild Strawberry
Fraisier des bois
Wald-Erdbeere
Fresa salvaje
Fragola di bosco
Bosaardbei

A *Lactuca sativa*
Lettuce
Laitue cultivée
Gartensalat
Lechuga
Lattuga
Sla

B *Eruca vesicaria ssp. sativa*
Garden Rocket
Roquette
Garten-Senfrauke
Rúcula
Rucola

C *Ocimum basilicum*
Basil
Basilic
Basilikum
Albahaca
Basilico
Basilicum

D *Cichorium intybus var. foliosum*
Italian Chicory
Cichorium intybus : endive
Chicorée
Achicoria roja
Radicchio
Witlof

E *Tropaeolum majus*
Garden nasturtium
Grande Capucine
Kapuzinerkresse
Capuchina
Nasturzio comune
Oost-Indische kers

397

A *Rumex sanguineus*
Sorrel
Oseille
Hain-Ampfer
Rumex
Lapazio
Bloedzuring

B *Oreganum*
Oregano
Orpin de l'Orégon
Oregano
Orégano
Origano
Marjolein

C *Eruca vesicaria
ssp. Sativa*
Garden Rocket
Roquette cultivée
Garten-Senfrauke
Rúcula
Rucola

D *Crataegus*
Hawthorn
Aubépine
Weißdorn
Crataegus
Biancospino
Meidoorn

E *Petroselinum*
Parsley
Persil
Petersilie
Perejil
Prezzemolo
Peterselie

F *Sanguisorba minor*
Salad Burnet
Pimprenelle
Kleiner Wiesenknopf
Pimpinela menor
Pimpinella
Kleine pimpernel

Staffordshire, UK

A *Matteuccia struthiopteris*
Ostrich fern
Fougère allemande
Straußenfarn
Matteuccia struthiopteris
Felce penna di struzzo
Struisvaren

B *Hosta*
Plantain Lilly
Hosta
Herzblattlilie
Planta de lidia
Hosta
Hartlelie

A *Mentha*
Mint
Menthe
Minze
Menta
Menta
Munt

B *Sempervivum*
Houseleek
Joubarbe
Hauswurz
Siemprevivas
Semprevivo
Huislook

C *Myosotis*
Forget-me-not
Myosotis
Vergissmeinnicht
Nomeolvides
Nontiscordardimé
Vergeet-mij-nietje

A *Mentha*
Mint
Menthe
Minze
Menta
Menta
Munt

B *Helichrysum italicum*
Curry Plant
Immortelle d'Italie
Currykraut
Flor de papel
Elicriso
Strobloem

C *Petroselinum crispum*
Parsley
Persil frisé
Petersilie
Perejil
Prezzemolo
Peterselie

D *Rosmarinus officinalis*
Rosemary
Romarin
Rosmarin
Romero
Rosmarino
Rozemarijn

E *Origanum vulgare*
Oregano
Origan
Oregano
Orégano común
Origano comune
Wilde marjolein

F *Lathyrus odoratus*
Sweet Pea
Pois de senteur
Duftende Platterbse
Guisante de olor
Cicerchia odorosa
Reukerwt

G *Salvia farinacea*
Mealy Sage
Sauge farineuse bleue
Mehliger Salbei
Sálvia-farinhenta
Salvia blu
Meelsalie

H *Dianthus barbatus*
Sweet William
Œillet
Bartnelke
Clavel
Garofano dei poeti
Duizendschoon

I *Verbena bonariensis*
Argentinian Vervain
Verveine de Buenos-Aires
Argentinisches Eisenkraut
Verbena púrpura
Verbena di Buenos Aires
Stijf ijzerhard

J *Cosmos*
Schmuckkörbchen
Cosmea

K *Rosa 'Pink Tiara'*
Rose
Rosier
Roos

L *Veronicastrum*
Culver's root
Véronique
Kandelaber-Ehrenpreis
Veronicastrum
Radice di Culver
Ereprijs

M *Thymus*
Thyme
Thym
Thymian
Tomillo común
Timo comune
Echte tijm

A *Sedum rupestre*
Jenny's Stonecrop
Orpin des rochers
Felsen-Fetthenne
Uñas de gato
Borracina rupestre
Tripmadam

B *Aucuba japonica 'Variegata'*
Japanese Laurel
Acuba du Japon
Japanische Aukube
Laurel motedao
Alloro giapponese
Broodboom

C *Petunia*
Pétunia
Petunie

D *Rheum rhabarbarum*
Rhubarb
Rhubarbe
Rhabarber
Ruibarbo
Rabarbaro
Rabarber

A *Bacopa monnieri 'Snowflake'*

Water Hyssop

Hysope d'eau

Kleines Fettblatt/ Brahmi

Bacopa

B *Allium 'Red Mohican'*

Allium

Ail d'ornement

Zierlauch

Ajo ornamental

Aglio ornamentale

Sierui

C *Pennisetum glaucum 'Purple Majesty'*

Pearl Millet

Mil à chandelle

Rohrkolbenhirse

Mijo perla

Miglio perlato

Lampenpoetsersgras

D *Calibrachoa 'Can-Can Black Cherry'*
Million Bells
Calibrachoa
Zauberglöckchen
Petunia calibrachoa
Petunia nana
Minipetunia

E *Glechoma hederacea 'Variegata'*
Ground-Ivy
Lierre terrestre
Gundermann
Hiedra terrestre
Edera terrestre
Hondsdraf

F *Ipomoea batatas 'Bright Ideas Black'*
Sweet Potato
Patate douce
Süßkartoffel
Batata
Patata dolce
Zoete aardappel

A *Galanthus nivalis*
Snowdrop
Perce-neige
Schneeglöckchen
Galanto
Bucaneve
Sneeuwklokje

B *Sedum rupestre*
Jenny's Stonecrop
Orpin des rochers
Felsen-Fetthenne
Uñas de gato
Borracina rupestre
Tripmadam

C *Sempervivum*
Houseleek
Joubarbe
Hauswurz
Siemprevivas
Semprevivo
Huislook

Collections
Sammlungen
Colecciones
Collezioni
Collecties

A *Centranthus ruber*
Red Valerian
Centranthe rouge
Rote Spornblume
Milamores
Valeriana rossa
Spoorbloem

B *Ocimum basilicum*
Basil
Basilic
Basilikum
Albahaca
Basilico
Basilicum

C *Hydrangea macrophylla*
Hydrangea
Hortensia
Hortensie
Ortensia dei fioristi

D *Zinnia*
Zinnie

Melon 1875
Duke of Edinburgh
a large size handsome Melon
Pale green skin netted
Rather thick skin

1873
Malvern Hall Melon
Very good green flesh medeum size
Very thin Skin

1873
Bromham Hall Melon
Larger then Malvern Hall
is a good but not extra fine melon
Fine flavour but thick skin

30 Seeds 1889
Golden Perfection
Melon
Very thin Skin — Very fine fruit
7 lb 15 ounces
Penzlton
Aug 28/89

On 1st March Plant
three Seeds in 3
Separate pots, one
in each pot in
a Hot Bed; When
large enough plant
them out in the
Vinery in the old
under the Hot water
pipes & let them run
over the ground under
the vines & half.

St Clement
Graie
a very large american
Gourd

Monro's Little Heath Melon, Seed 1874

Monro's
Little Heath Melon
From a fruit 6½ lb weight grown 1874
This is a fine flavoured Scarlet flesh melon and
grows to a large Size say from 4 lb to 6½ lb
weight, 6 or 8 fruit on each plant will run to that
Size. It is ribbed & round fruit must not be
but is very thin skinned.

Oval Shaped Melon
Yellow when ripe. From Foreign
Seed Very thin skin & fine flavour
Saved at Penzlton on
August 29/86

Cirencester Prize Hybrid 1882
weighed 5 lb fine flavour thin skin a
very fine & handsome melon long shape
& beautifully netted. Aug 1882

A *Agapanthus 'Midnight Star'*
African Lily
Agapanthe
Schmucklilie
Lirio africano
Agapanto
Afrikaanse lelie

B *Yucca*
Palmlilie
Yuca
Palmlelie

Essex, UK

A *Salvia*
Common Sage
Sauge officinale
Salbei
Salvia común
Salvia comune
Echte salie

B *Brassica oleracea var. palmifolia 'Cavolo Nero'*
Lacinato Kale
Chou palmier
Palmkohl
Col rizada de la Toscana
Cavolo
Palmkool

C *Ligustrum*
Privet
Troène
Liguster
Ligustro

D *Digitalis purpurea*
Foxglove
Digitale pourpre
Roter Fingerhut
Dedalera
Digitale rossa
Vingerhoedskruid

E *Hedera helix*
Ivy
Lierre grimpant
Efeu
Hiedra común
Edera comune
Klimop

F *Allium schoenoprasum*
Chives
Ciboulette
Schnittlauch
Cebollino
Erba cipollina
Bieslook

Keukenhof, Lisse, Netherlands

A *Galanthus nivalis*
Snowdrop
Perce-neige
Schneeglöckchen
Galanto
Bucaneve
Sneeuwklokje

Dorset, UK

433

Essex, UK

Hampton Court
Flower Show,
London, UK

Retreats
Refuges
Rückzugsorte
Retiros
Luoghi di ritiro
Toevluchtsoorden

Surrey, UK

Chelsea Flower
Show, London, UK

Gloucestershire, UK

Cape Town,
South Africa

Wiltshire, UK

447

France

Lincolnshire,UK

New York City, USA

Caledon, Canada

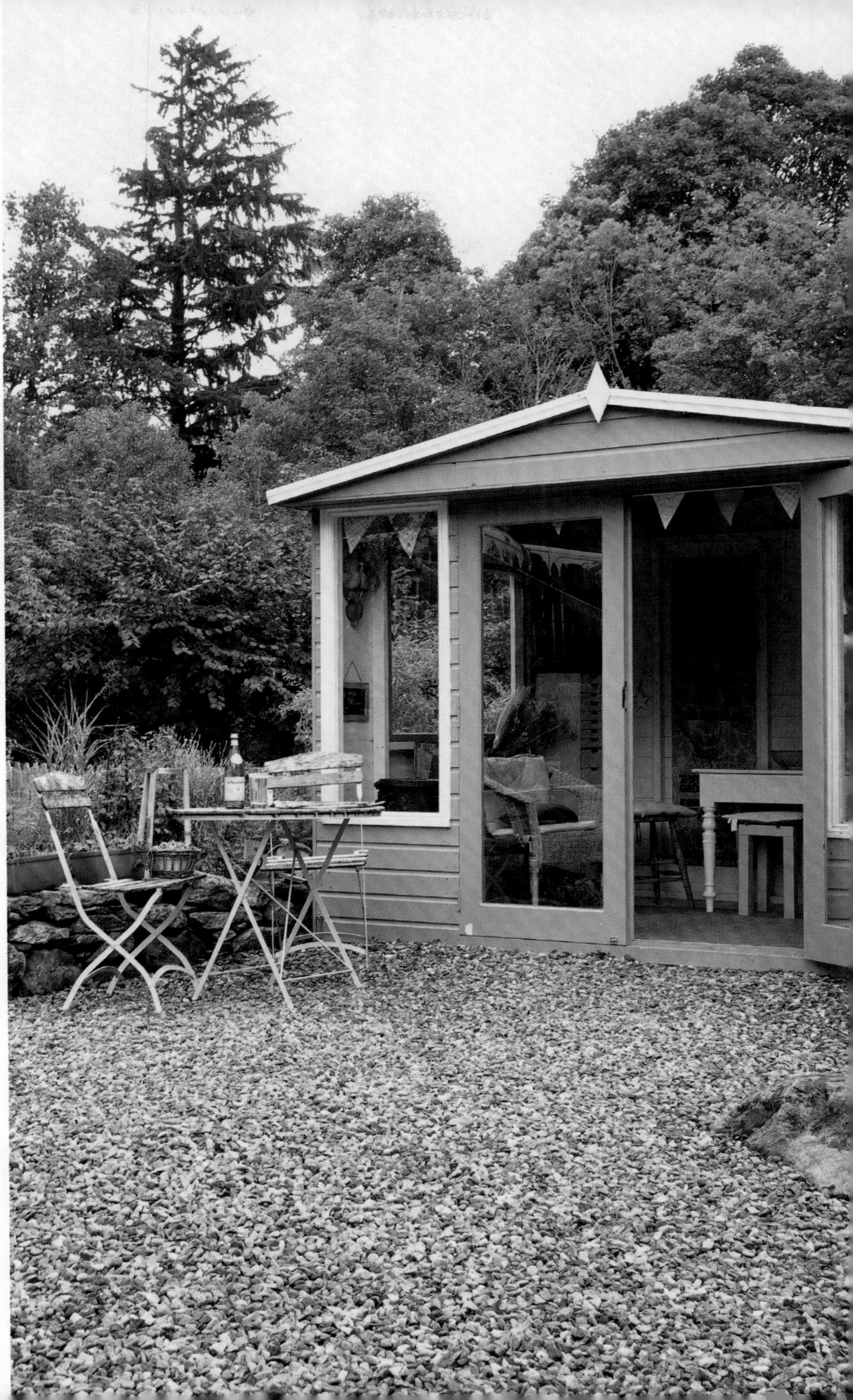

Wijland, Netherlands

London, UK

Bordeaux, France

Gloucestershire, UK

London, UK

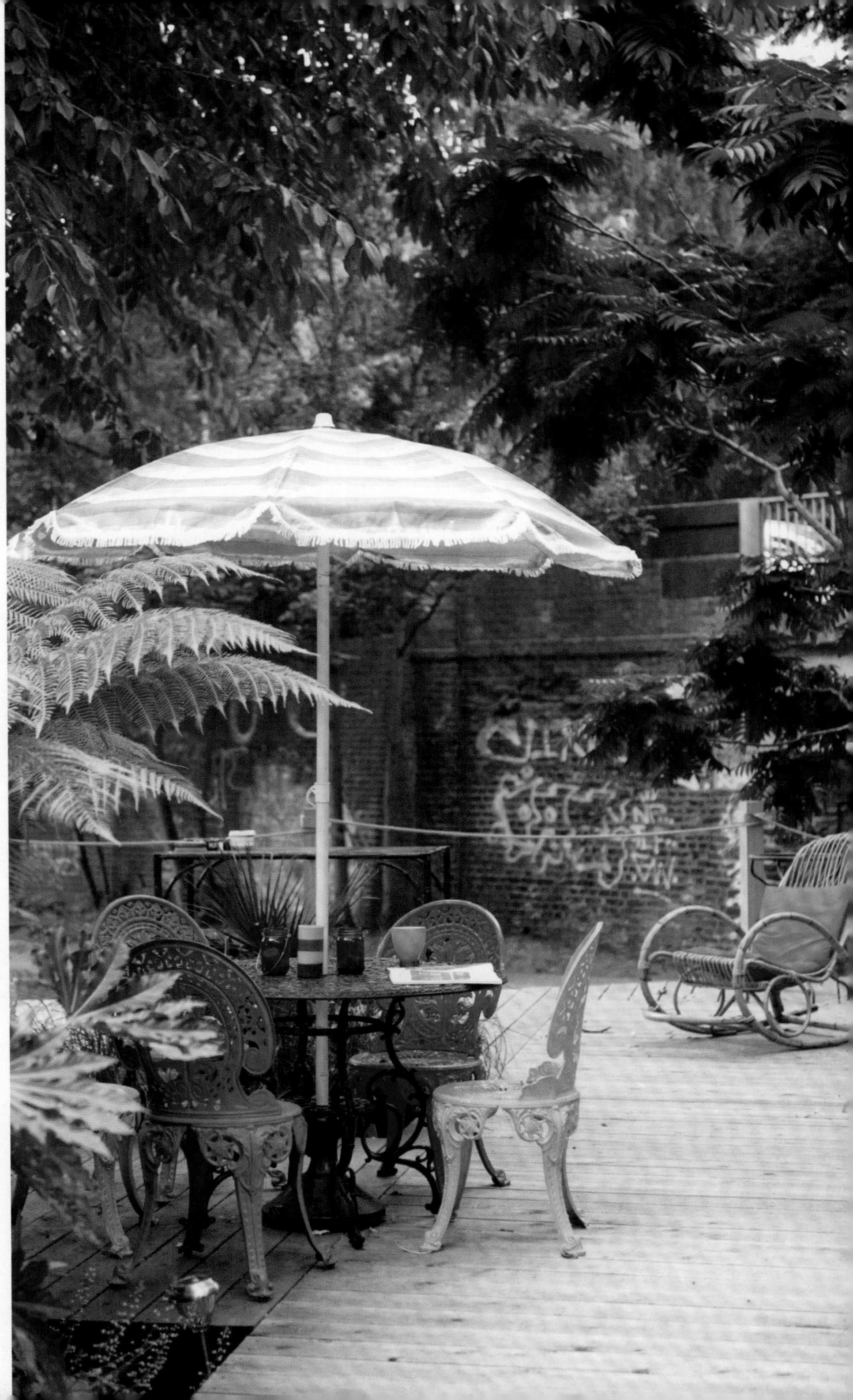

London, UK

London, UK

London, UK

Oxfordshire, UK

Yorkshire, UK

Manchester, UK

Essex, UK

Hampshire, UK

Cumbria, UK

The Cape Winelands, South Africa

Mabic; 237, 238 Nicola Stocken; 239 David Tull; 240 Richard Wareham; 241 Nicola Stocken; 242, 243 Perry Mastrovito; 244 Nicola Stocken; 245 Charles Hawes, Design: Alistair W Baldwin. Sponsor: Welcome to Yorkshire; 246, 247 Anna Omiotek-Tott; 248 Annie Green-Armytage, Design: Sadie May Stowell – Sponsor: Brand USA; 249 Anna Omiotek-Tott, Design: Jamie Langlands; 250 Jerry Pavia; 251 Nicola Stocken; 252 Jenny Lilly, Design: Jekka McVicar, Sponsor: St John's Hospice; 253 Heather Edwards, Design: Jamie Langlands; 254 Richard Wareham; 256/257 Brent Wilson; 258 Perry Mastrovito; 259 Brent Wilson; 260 Nicola Stocken; 262 Graham Strong; 263 J S Sira; 264/265 Nicola Stocken; 266, 267 John Glover; 269 John Glover. Design: Pamela Woods; 270 John Glover, Design: Anne Frith; 271–273 Nicola Stocken; 274/275 Brent Wilson; 276/277 Anna Omiotek-Tott; 278 Rob Whitworth, Location: The Lebanese Courtyard, Chelsea FS 2006; 279 GAP Photos; 280 Juliette Wade; 281 Victoria Firmston; 282/283 Hanneke Reijbroek, Chaumont sur Loire 2014; 284 Jonathan Buckley, Design: Sarah Mead, Yeo Valley Garden; 285, 286 GAP Photos; 287 Fiona Lea; 288 GAP Photos; 289 Nicola Stocken; 290 Janet Johnson; 291 Jenny Lilly, Design: Burlish Park Primary School; 292 GAP Photos; 293 Mark Bolton; 294 Hanneke Reijbroek, Location: Keukenhof, Lisse, Holland; 295 GAP Photos; 296 Robert Mabic; 297 Richard Wareham; 298 Robert Mabic; 299 Victoria Firmston; 300 Martin Hughes-Jones; 301 Clive Nichols, KEUKENHOF GARDENS, HOLLAND; 302 Marcus Harpur, Designer: Sean Murray Sponsor: Royal Horticultural Society; 303 Stephen Studd, Designer: Sean Murray Sponsor: Royal Horticultural Society; 304 Graham Strong; 305 Hanneke Reijbroek, Location: Dutch Design Week/Strijp-S/Eindhoven Holland. Design: 5DSolutions/Paul van Hedel ; 306 GAP Photos; 307 Robert Mabic,Design: Kate Turner; 308/309 S & O; 310 Michael Howes;

311 Costas Picadas; 312/313 Carole Drake, courtesy Ian Willis; 314 Dan Duchars; 315 Jenny Lilly; 316 Julia Boulton; 317 Graham Strong; 318 Pat Tuson; 319 Fiona Lea; 320/321 Fiona Lea; 322 Leigh Clapp, Little Orchards, Nic Howard; 323 Hanneke Reijbroek; 324 Jenny Lilly, Design: Ben Corah; 325 Ron Evans; 326 Nicola Stocken, Dial Park; 328, 329 Fiona Lea; 330 Nicola Stocken, Dial Park; 331 Nicola Stocken; 332, 333 Lee Beel, Garden: The Court, North Ferriby, Yorkshire; 334 John Glover; 335 GAP Photos; 336 Anna Omiotek-Tott, Design: Graham Bodle – Gold and Best Fresh Garden; 337 Robert Mabic; 338, 339 Nicola Stocken; 340, 341 GAP Photos; 342/243 Fiona Lea; 344 John Glover; 345 Robert Mabic; 346 Graham Strong; 347 Fiona Lea; 348, 349 GAP Photos; 350/351 Jerry Pavia; 352 Torie Chugg; 353 Nicola Stocken; 354 Anna Omiotek-Tott; 355 Clive Nichols, Keukenhof Gardens, Holland; 356 Liz Every; 357 Victoria Firmston; 358 Robert Mabic; 359 GAP Photos; 360 Paul Debois; 361 Michael Howes; 362 Douglas Gibb; 363 Pernilla Bergdahl; 364–367 Nicola Stocken; 368 Gary Smith; 369 Robert Mabic; 370/371 Colin Poole; 372 Tria Giovan; 373 Lynn Keddie; 374/375 Graham Strong; 376 Jerry Pavia; 377 Nicola Stocken; 378 GAP Photos; 380, 381 Heather Edwards, Design: David Domoney; 382 Graham Strong; 383, 384 Jerry Pavia; 385 Gary Smith; 386 Julia Boulton; 387 GAP Photos; 388 Lynn Keddie; 389 Jerry Pavia; 390 Julia Boulton; 391 GAP Photos; 392 J S Sira; 393 GAP Photos; 394 Graham Strong; 395 Julia Boulton; 396, 397 Graham Strong; 398, 399 GAP Photos; 400–403 Nicola Stocken; 404 Graham Strong; 405 Suzie Gibbons; 406 Brent Wilson; 407 Nicola Stocken; 408 Julia Boulton; 409 Jenny Lilly; 410 GAP Photos; 411 Nicola Stocken; 412 Julia Boulton; 413 GAP Photos; 414 Jerry Harpur, Design: Cary Wolinsky ; 416, 417 Julia Boulton; 418, 419 Nicola Stocken; 420, 421 Suzie Gibbons, Design: Martin Scorey; 422 Nicola Stocken; 423 Rachel Warne – Woolcott & Smith Courtyard

garden London; 424 Nadia Mackenzie; 425 Suzie Gibbons, DESIGN HELEN RICHES; 426 Lynn Keddie; 427 Julia Boulton; 428, 429 Hanneke Reijbroek, Location: Keukenhof, Lisse, Holland; 430 Clive Nichols, Garden: Bryan's Ground; 431 Julia Boulton; 432 Jerry Pavia; 433 Carole Drake; 434 GAP Photos; 435 Gary Smith; 436 Jerry Pavia; 437 J S Sira, Design: Capital Growth; 438/439 Colin Poole; 440 Colin Poole; 441 Nicola Stocken; 442/443 Jacqui Hurst, Design: Ann-Marie Powell; 444 House & Leisure,H&L/W.HEATH, www. hemingwayhouse.co.za; 445 Amanda Turner; 446 House & Leisure – H&L, J. DE VILLIERS; 447 Amanda Turner; 448/449 Benjamin Mamet; 450 Costas Picadas; 451 Amanda Knox; 452/453 Robin Stubbert; 454, 455 Douglas Gibb; 456/457 Hanneke Reijbroek, www.inhetwijland.nl; 458 Julien Fernandez; 459 Dan Duchars; 460/461 Amanda Turner; 462, 463 Ingrid Rasmussen, Emily Wheeler www.blonstein.co.uk; 464 Spike Powell; 465 Dan Duchars; 466 Ingrid Rasmussen; 467 Rachael Smith, Victoria Tunstall, De Fire Arstider ; 468 Ingrid Rasmussen, www. rennaissancelondon.com; 469 Colin Poole; 470 Lee Avison; 471 Lee Beel, Garden: The Court, North Ferriby, Yorkshire; 472 Dan Duchars; 473 Howard Rice; 474/475 Leigh Clapp,The Thatched Cottage, Hampshire NGS; 476 Robin Stubbert www.pinesamplerfurniture.com ; 477 Carole Drake, Garden: Askham Hall, Penrith, Cumbria; 478 Bureaux, Photographs: Greg Cox – Production: Retha Erichsen

Front cover: see p. 304
Back cover: see p.191